T0113913

THE
GLORIOUS MILLENNIAL KINGDOM

PHILIP ALAN KLUMPP

WESTBOW
PRESS®
A DIVISION OF THOMAS NELSON
& ZONDERVAN

Copyright © 2021 Philip Alan Klumpp.

All rights reserved. No part of this book may be used or reproduced by any means, graphic, electronic, or mechanical, including photocopying, recording, taping or by any information storage retrieval system without the written permission of the author except in the case of brief quotations embodied in critical articles and reviews.

This book is a work of non-fiction. Unless otherwise noted, the author and the publisher make no explicit guarantees as to the accuracy of the information contained in this book and in some cases, names of people and places have been altered to protect their privacy.

WestBow Press books may be ordered through booksellers or by contacting:

WestBow Press
A Division of Thomas Nelson & Zondervan
1663 Liberty Drive
Bloomington, IN 47403
www.westbowpress.com
844-714-3454

Because of the dynamic nature of the Internet, any web addresses or links contained in this book may have changed since publication and may no longer be valid. The views expressed in this work are solely those of the author and do not necessarily reflect the views of the publisher, and the publisher hereby disclaims any responsibility for them.

Any people depicted in stock imagery provided by Getty Images are models, and such images are being used for illustrative purposes only.
Certain stock imagery © Getty Images.

Interior Image Credit: Katie Elisabeth Brock (Images 1-3), Logos Bible Software for Image 4

ISBN: 978-1-6642-4757-4 (sc)
ISBN: 978-1-6642-4759-8 (hc)
ISBN: 978-1-6642-4758-1 (e)

Library of Congress Control Number: 2021921372

Print information available on the last page.

WestBow Press rev. date: 10/28/2021

Unless otherwise indicated, all scripture taken from the New King James Version®. Copyright © 1982 by Thomas Nelson. Used by permission. All rights reserved.

Scripture quotations marked (ESV) are from The ESV® Bible (The Holy Bible, English Standard Version®), copyright © 2001 by Crossway, a publishing ministry of Good News Publishers. Used by permission. All rights reserved.

Scripture quotations marked (NIV) are taken from the Holy Bible, New International Version®, NIV®. Copyright © 1973, 1978, 1984, 2011 by Biblica, Inc.® Used by permission of Zondervan. All rights reserved worldwide. www.zondervan.com The "NIV" and "New International Version" are trademarks registered in the United States Patent and Trademark Office by Biblica, Inc.®

Scripture quotations marked (NLT) are taken from the Holy Bible, New Living Translation, copyright ©1996, 2004, 2015 by Tyndale House Foundation. Used by permission of Tyndale House Publishers, a Division of Tyndale House Ministries, Carol Stream, Illinois 60188. All rights reserved.

Acknowledgments

Mrs. Barbara A. Klumpp: encouraging wife, mentor, and advisor, North Tonawanda, New York

Mrs. Katie E. (Klumpp) Brock: graphic artist, Mechanicsburg, Pennsylvania

Ms. Methuselah C. Ramos: encouraging manuscript editor

Mrs. Erma C. (Cordero) Ramos: encouraging manuscript reader, Cebu City, Philippines

Rev. Richard W. Gilbert: encouraging theological advisor, Lewiston, New York

Mrs. Evelyn Marie Ellisen: permission for Appendix 2

Mr. David Charles Ellisen: son of author, Saint Helens, Oregon

CONTENTS

TESTIMONY

My interest in prophecy began when I was a child. I am the youngest of four boys, and I grew up on a village farm in western New York. My parents, Walter and Alice Klumpp, were devout born-again Christians and charter members of the Grace Baptist Church of Newfane, New York. They faithfully took us to church, and we learned that Jesus could return at any time. My mother led me to Christ at age of fourteen, right before my New York State Regents Math exam.

My father promised the Lord to send each of his sons to Bible school, so they could study the scriptures and put that knowledge into practice. We four brothers attended Bible college, and three of us became foreign missionaries, serving in Mexico, Colombia, and the Philippines. Our oldest brother was active at the Grace Bible Church in Newfane, and he helped support us in the mission field. You can read our story about growing up on a small village farm and later moving on to serve in faraway countries in my first book, *The Tale of Four Brothers*.

I met my future wife, Barbara Anne Cooper, in the summer of 1976, at the Niagara Bible Conference, where our family served for many years. Barb was the missionary speaker for the children's camp. She planned to go to Hong Kong as a missionary nurse. We fell in love and shared our common burden to become foreign missionaries.

The Lord called us to serve together in the Philippines, and we arrived there as newlyweds on July 5, 1978. We flew over the

Continental Date Line during the United States of America's Fourth of July celebration. The Philippines had been a colonial territory of the US and had celebrated the Fourth of July as "Philippine-American Friendship Day." It was an appropriate day for our arrival.

More than forty years have passed since we became missionaries with ABWE International. Barb and I have served in a mission hospital, doing evangelism, planting churches, and teaching in various seminaries.

We spent our first four-year term of ministry learning the Cebuano language and working with the Filipino staff at the Leyte Baptist Hospital. Barb served as a nurse, and I filled in as administrator/overseer of the evangelists and maintenance personnel. We loved using the local dialect in preaching and witnessing to patients who came for medical consultation.

In our second and third terms of service, we planted the Grace Baptist Church of Baybay, Leyte. It is an hour up the road from the hospital. In 1990, the church had a Filipino pastor in place to carry on the ministry.

During this time, I received a master's degree in religious education (MRE) from the Asia Biblical Theological Seminary (connected to Cornerstone University in Grand Rapids, Michigan). My final thesis was on urban church planting in the Philippines. I surveyed Cebu City and asked other evangelical groups if ABWE missionaries would be welcome to start a ministry in that metropolis of one million people. All were favorable, and we began the pioneering work in 1991. Over that next term of service, Grace Baptist Church of Cebu City became independent under Filipino leadership and continued evangelism and outreach efforts. Since then, the Filipino leadership has had a vision for the whole island of Cebu. Outreach pastors are now planting daughter churches in various stages of independence. We praise the Lord that they have carried the torch to take Jesus's Great Commission to the ends of the earth.

Since the late 1990s, Barb and I have taught in various Bible schools and seminaries in the Philippines. From 2007 to 2018, we taught at the Bukidnon Fundamental Baptist Seminary (BFBS) on the southern island of Mindanao. The students we taught have taken positions as youth pastors, music directors, teachers, and local pastors of congregations. We echo the apostle Paul's praise: "For you are our glory and joy ... a crown of rejoicing" (1 Thessalonians 2:19–20). The Lord God has been so gracious to Barb and me in allowing us to serve as missionaries with our Filipino brethren. It was at BFBS that I taught the Major and Minor Prophets and studied the truths that have become the basis for this book.

We raised our two children, Andrew and Katie, in the Philippines. They are both married and living in Pennsylvania. We have two granddaughters whom we visit as often as we can. We pray for them to be God's messengers to the next generation.

I pray that you will be as eager as I am for the return of the Lord Jesus to reign as King on the earth (1 John 3:2). May you grow in excitement for His return as you read *The Glorious Millennial Kingdom*.

INTRODUCTION

Researching for this book was, for me, an experience beyond compare. Preparing and teaching this material has touched my heart, and I trust it will touch yours also. This book provides assurance and hope in the revelation of what God will do in the marvelous Second Advent of our Lord Jesus Christ.

God has allowed me to serve as a missionary, teaching in the Philippines for the past forty years. One of my assignments was teaching the Major and Minor Prophets of the Old Testament. As I taught my third-year students at the Bukidnon Fundamental Baptist Seminary (undergraduate) in the Philippines, I was impressed with the volume of information the Lord God has revealed about His grace in drawing His chosen people, Israel, to Himself. God's passion for His children is to restore them to a showcase of His glory. He wants His people to someday live in His Holy Land of Israel with their Messiah Jesus as the "King of kings and Lord of lords" (Revelation 19:16).

In the 1970s, when I was studying at Washington Bible College, prophecy and eschatology were emphasized as part of the curriculum. At that time, churches often held seminars and conferences about the "Last Days." Today, people are again asking questions about the future. His return is the "Blessed Hope" that we all are waiting for (Titus 2:13). I hope you enjoy this refreshing and thrilling study as we wait for His return.

In *The Glorious Millennial Kingdom*, we will study specifically what the earth will be like when Jesus and His saints rule and reign from Jerusalem. I embrace, along with many other biblical scholars, the eschatological "premillennial" view of Christ's second return. In other words, Christ Jesus will come back to earth and will rule on earth for a literal one thousand years. The thousand years that Jesus reigns on earth are called the "Millennium" or the "Millennial Kingdom." The beginning chapters of this book emphasize the promise of the "Marriage Supper of the Lamb," referred to in Revelation 19:7–9 and Matthew 22:1–14; 24:30–31. There will be a glorious reception and coronation of the coming King, Jesus.

Everyone loves a wedding. Family and friends want to witness the marriage of a couple they may have known for a long time. The bride and groom have made extensive preparations for the day of their wedding, and we especially look forward to attending their reception. The master of ceremonies will introduce the happily married couple. Many will join in the festivities with food, fellowship, and wishes for many happy years to come. It is a grand and glorious event that will especially honor the bride and groom.

There will be a wonderful time at the beginning of the Millennial Kingdom to honor King Jesus and His Bride. His "Bride" are the saints of the Church Age:

> Christ also loved the Church and gave Himself for her, that He might sanctify and cleanse her … by the Word, that He might present her to Himself a glorious Church. (Ephesians 5:25b –27)

Jesus Christ, our Lord, will be exalted on His rightful throne. In this coronation of King Jesus, He will have His Bride, "the Church," surrounding Him with radiant splendor (Revelation 19:7–8). It is God who will do all this, and we, as born-again believers, will be His Bride.

Charles H. Gabriel, the beloved hymn writer, wrote, "When all my labors and trials are o'er, and I am safe on that beautiful shore, just to be near the dear Lord I adore will through the ages be glory for me. O that will be, glory for me, glory for me, glory for me; when by His grace, I shall look on His face, that will be glory, be glory for me."[1]

When we, as true believers, see Jesus's face, "we shall be like Him, for we shall see Him as He is" (1 John 3:2). Indeed, that will be glory for you and me! I am excited that I will see my Lord Jesus face-to-face, and I hope you are too.

Christ's Bride and the faithful saints of all ages will live, rule, and reign with Christ in His Kingdom (2 Timothy 2:12a). Revelation 21:3 states that He will dwell with men and will be their God. It starts with Jesus as King in His millennial reign with men on earth, and it will continue in the New Jerusalem for all eternity (Revelation 21–22).

The last days of our world, with its tribulations, will climax with Jesus judging all evil. He will put away the old and start anew with His thousand-year Kingdom on earth. I will be there! The Holy Scriptures have promised! You will be there also if you have put your trust in Jesus as your personal Savior and Lord. Are you excited to be with Jesus in His Kingdom to come?

My prayer is that this book will also help us understand the flow of events before Christ Jesus's coronation and the "Marriage Supper of the Lamb." At this feast, the world and saints of all times will see Jesus's radiance with His Bride. It will be the beginning of all genuine believers ruling and reigning with Jesus in making everything new in His Kingdom. I pray that with awe and excitement, you will feel the pulse of the prophetic truth of God's Word ringing out in your mind.

I have included quotes from several commentators indented for clarification of the context of the Holy Scriptures. I also incorporate my explanation of transitional events of prophetic eschatology of Christ's millennial rule.

Of course, with the help of the commentators, I make separate paragraphs in the text with my opinion of what may very well happen in the manifestation of Christ as King. I also ask stimulating questions to engage you, the reader, in the excitement as we look forward to living in the time of Christ's glorious Millennial Kingdom.

the MARRIAGE SUPPER OF THE Lamb

CHAPTER 1

THE BEGINNING EXCITEMENT OF CHRIST'S MILLENNIAL KINGDOM

When the Son of Man comes in His glory, and all the holy
angels with Him, then He will sit on the throne of His glory.
—Matthew 25:31

The Anticipation of Christ's Kingdom

When was the last time you anticipated something exciting in your life? Was it a recent birthday, wedding, honeymoon, or well-needed vacation? "Hooray! When are we going to get there?" "How many days till my birthday?" "Is it almost Christmas?" Children get excited and express their anticipation with repetitive questions. Anticipation mounts for adults as well as children!

The Excitement for Christ's Return

In your relationship with God, do you look forward to His return with great enthusiasm and anticipation? The Millennial Kingdom will be where our Lord Jesus Christ will become the

King, and we, as His Church, will be the Bride. He will rule and reign from His throne in Jerusalem. The day of Christ's return will be spectacular. We will see the beauty and majesty of our Savior and King as God's fulfillment of His divine glory and splendor. "When will we get there?" "When will He return?" I hope that, as you read this book, you will feel the expectancy of a future climax of the reign of our Savior and Lord.

In the events leading up to the Millennium, the first phase of His return is called "the Rapture." At the Rapture, we genuine Christians will meet Jesus in the clouds to enter God's heaven (1 Thessalonians 4:13–18). Those who are left behind on earth will experience the seven-year Tribulation time.

The Tribulation will be a time of great trouble and turmoil on the earth. Satan will attempt to thwart the works of God. During that time, many antichrists will come to confuse and deceive the peoples of the world. There will be one actual impostor of the living Christ, mentioned in prophecy as being the "Antichrist" (Matthew 24:5; Daniel 7:20; Revelation 13:6–7). He makes peace for a while and later breaks his treaty with Israel to defile the Temple of God in the holy city of Jerusalem. The turmoil of these events is presented to us by the Old Testament prophet Daniel and the apostle John's writings in the book of Revelation.

The Excitement for the End-Time Prophecies

This book will show the excellence of what our Sovereign God will bring to fulfillment in the end-times. Jesus Christ will literally come to the earth, as the Bible has said. Many prophetic events will lead up to the supreme millennial rule of our Lord and King. The events of the inaugural placement of the King on His rightful throne will be spectacular. When God does something great, perfect, and glorious, it will be more than we can imagine.

In the Millennial Kingdom and the rule of Jesus Christ, there will be references from the Old Testament writings mixed with references from the New Testament. The last book of the Bible is the apostle John's book of "The Revelation," yet even it does not reveal all the details of the millennial reign of Christ. The psalms of praise and adoration to the citadel of Jerusalem also give much hope to the everlasting supremacy of a deserved King (Psalm 45:6).

There is a combination of various pockets of verses, information, and foretelling of events of the Millennium. Even at the birth of Jesus, Mary's husband, Joseph, is mentioned as "the son of David." The genealogy of Joseph's linage gives King Jesus the rightful place to sit on David's throne (Matthew 1:20). The Old Testament prophets wrote other various prophecies stating that Jesus will be the Supreme Ruler on Mount Zion (Micah 4:7, 10, 11, 13; Isaiah 9:6–7).

In the following chapters, many Old Testament prophetic passages will be combined with Jesus's Mount Olivet discourse to bring about the information about the Millennial Kingdom. The Bible reveals in its context and hermeneutical interpretation precisely what God wants us to know. All scripture must be studied and compared to conclude what God intended. You, as a reader, and I, as the presenter of the prophecies, will find what will most likely happen in the Millennial Kingdom of King Jesus.

Students and researchers of the Holy Scriptures combine what is foretold from the Old Testament, Jesus's teachings in the Gospels, and the promises of the New Testament revelations of the end-times. We have a beautiful picture and description of future events that will be unfolded before us. The fulfillment of prophecy is our hope for a blessed and peaceful future with the "Lord of lords and King of kings" (Revelation19:16). The presence of God and His words of prophecy will work all things together for His highest glory in bringing Christ Jesus, God's Son, to His rightful throne. He will rule in His thousand-year kingdom on this earth.

The Excitement over Premillennial Events

This research will present the events that lead up to Christ Jesus sitting on His throne in the Millennial Kingdom. His reign is the center of the world's affairs in Jerusalem. His coronation will be the climax as He becomes the victor over the terrible and troublesome times for the Jewish people and Christians alike at the end of the seven-year Tribulation. It will be a time of God's judgment upon the world system of its day. There will be no ideal human government system that will have precedence to rule on the earth. Plato once said, "The best ruling governmental system is a benevolent king and monarch that will bring the wisest judgment and justice to all peoples." The Millennial Kingdom can only accomplish peace that Jesus, the Lord and King, will set up. Oh, what we can look forward to in anticipation of true worship, service, and glory to the King of kings. Blessed be the name of the Lord, the King over any other kings of the earth!

Can you imagine with me the actual moment when Jesus Christ reveals Himself? His Second Advent will be the fulfillment of His return to the Mount of Olives (Acts 1:9–12). After Jesus ascended to heaven, the angel said, "This same Jesus, who was taken up from you into heaven, will so come in like manner as you saw Him go into heaven" (v. 11). Just imagine! You probably have heard of the battle of Armageddon (Revelation 16:16). The Lord Jesus uses the sharp sword that proceeds from His mouth to bring a death penalty upon His enemies. Destruction and defeat of his enemies will be by the words of His mouth (Revelation 19:5–21). I wonder if Jesus will circle on His white spectacular kingly horse in splendor and glory. Perhaps Jesus's appearance will be magnified in our eyes as we gaze upon Him.

The Approaching Day of the Christ Jesus's Glorious Revelation of Himself

TV Cameras on the Beginning Events

At a given time, there will be a gathering of various armies (Revelation 16:12-16). There will be a buildup of weaponry from all nations that the Antichrist will set up against Israel and Jerusalem. The location is approximately fifty-five kilometers north in the Valley of Megiddo. Mass media will cover all the events near the outskirts of the most Holy Mount. Some people may indeed remember the scriptures and have cameras ready for Jesus to return and touch down on Mount of Olives as was prophesied (Acts 1:9–12, Zechariah 14:4). People all over the world will watch their flat-screen TVs or mobile phones for the time when Jesus will step down on the earth. The glamour and glory of Jesus's majesty will be telecast repeatedly to all nations. According to Revelation 11:8–12, two witnesses will come alive from the dead. These scriptures say that the whole world will see the resurrection of the two men. Media today can cover news all over the world.

Many people around the world will be amazed to see Jesus touching his feet on the Holy Mount. Cameras will shift from the armies' attack from the north (with troubles of ransacked homes and stores in Jerusalem) to the return of Jesus on the Mount of Olives in a flash. Photographers will capture both events. They will get the facts to share with the entire world of Christ's Second Coming and the magnificence and fulfillment of prophecy.

Just imagine the larger-than-life display of Christ Jesus riding on the majestic "white horse." It will be dynamic and glorious to see Him enter the earth's atmosphere from heaven. I believe the enemy soldiers, world leaders, television crews, the Antichrist, and the false prophets of all religions will see this white stallion with Jesus riding on it. They will be in a state of bewilderment, wondering what

Jesus will do. His first purpose is to bring devastation, death, and destruction to the enemies of Israel (Revelation 19). Jesus, the King, will come at the perfect time. He will arrive at the exact time when His enemy waits for the final command of the Antichrist to destroy Jerusalem and other political strongholds of Israel.

Christ's Attack on Israel's Enemies

Before the Antichrist can give the word of a missile attack and storming the gates of Jerusalem, Christ will come and save His elect nation and people. Christ's judgment will fulfill the prophecies of the battle of Armageddon in Revelation 16. He will show Himself victorious in all glory and glamour in the sky above the glorious "Promised Land" (Daniel 8:9).

When Jesus finishes off the enemies to the north, He will probably circle Jerusalem several times with His heavenly saints. They will wear dazzling pure and crystal white linen, also riding on white horses (Revelation 19:14). Jesus and his saints will show the people that He has guarded them against the worst attack from the "evil one." Jesus will slowly hover over the Mount of Olives for His moment to descend on the holy Mount:

> Now I saw heaven opened and behold a white horse. And He who sat on him was called "Faithful and True," and in righteousness, He judges and makes war … He was clothed with a robe dipped in blood, and His name is called the "Word of God." The armies in heaven, clothed in fine linen, white and clean, followed Him on white horses … And He has on His robe and His thigh a name written: "King of kings and Lord of lords." (Revelation 19:11, 13, 14, 16)

What a scene to behold! This event will be breathtaking, to say the least, as Jesus judges His enemies. His glory and majesty will show His grandeur over His chosen capital city of Jerusalem. Praise be to the Lord, Most High! He will be honored and praised for the triumphant entry and exceptional care and protection He gives to His people.

CHAPTER 2

THE GLORIOUS ENTRANCE INTO THE GLAMOROUS KINGDOM

Then they will see the Son of Man coming in
a cloud with power and great glory.
—Luke 21:27

Jesus Christ's Return as He Promised

Jesus will someday reveal Himself on the Mount of Olives. He will get off His white stallion and descend to touch His feet on the earth (Zechariah 14:4). The angel prophesied, "This same Jesus, who was taken up from you into heaven, will so come in like manner as you have seen Him go (ascend) into heaven" (Acts 1:11).

The media will show Jesus's glorified body gently floating down to the earth below. The sparkles of the pure white stallion in the sky above will be spectacular to give Christ's glorious appearance a wonder above all wonders. The hosts of the heavenly saints will surround Christ and His horse (Revelation 19:11–16; Zechariah 14:5). The live telecast will show the people of Jerusalem and surrounding areas looking in amazement at the sight of Christ, proclaiming His victory over the powers of darkness to give light to a future everlasting Kingdom (Zechariah 14:6–7).

Christ's Return to the Mount of Olives

The Bible tells us clearly what will happen when Jesus's feet touch the Mount of Olives, just east of the capital city of Jerusalem. Zechariah 14:4 states that an earthquake will have a magnitude of power to split the mount. A valley of escape will open up to the east and to the west. As the earthquake happens, people will panic. Lives will be lost. Some will be buried alive in the debris and landslides. The magnitude of this earthquake would never have been experienced before in this location. This mighty tremor is the very last of its kind from the seven years of Tribulation. The earthquake is a fulfillment of prophecy at the start of the Millennial Kingdom (Zechariah 14:5).

In Ezekiel 47:1–12, we find that this valley will have a spring of water bubble up to flow east and west. The stream of water will come from the holy sanctuary and will divide into two separate directions. One stream will flow to the east down to the Jordan River, ending up in the Dead Sea. Then the other will have a simultaneous descent to the west to the Mediterranean Sea (Zechariah 14:8). These events surely will be marvelous to watch and experience at the beginning of Christ's Kingdom. In later chapters, we will discuss the matter of the "valley" and the "river flow of healing." In chapter 11, we will discuss "a river of life." Also, chapter 13 explains the "management of pharmaceutical medicines."

Perhaps, during the earthquake or right after, the white stallion will come down to pick up the Lord Jesus and take Him away from the dangers of the fallout of the earthquake. There will be judgments pending to establish His reign in Zion (Isaiah 9:7). Then, with some speculation, Jesus will be whisked away on His white horse again to prepare Himself as the Bridegroom ready for His Bride to be announced to the world.

Christ, the True Bridegroom

It is essential to give reliable sources and biblical background to the whole matter of Christ Jesus, our Lord, as "the Lamb of God who takes away the sin of the world" (John 1:29)! John the Baptist verbally expressed this concept of Jesus becoming the atoning sacrifice as "the Lamb of God." His prelude to the ministry of Christ Jesus paved the way for future revelations of God's plan for the ages. Jesus would be (and was) crucified for all sinners. Whoever believes in Him is reconciled back to God. John foretold that the Savior and Lamb of God "must increase, but I (John) must decrease" (John 3:30). Jesus's popularity would rise, and John's would decline. Are we giving due honor and glory to Jesus as the Lamb of God for our salvation?

Jesus Himself said that John the Baptist was the greatest of the prophets (Luke 7:28). John was a cousin and a friend of Jesus. He also proclaimed a future Bridegroom and Bride concept with Christ. John stood and rejoiced to hear the Bridegroom's voice:

He who has the bride is the bridegroom; but the friend of the bridegroom, who stands and hears him, rejoices greatly because of the bridegroom's (Jesus's) voice. Therefore, this joy of mine is fulfilled. (John 3:29)

He felt the prediction in his spirit. There will come a day when this will be fulfilled. Do you have a fulfilling joy that Christ is your Savior and Bridegroom who will come for you? I hope you get the thrill and are eager to see the Lord Jesus coming as King.

Christ's Marriage to the Bride

In the tradition of the Jewish culture, marriage was a three-step process.

1. In the Old and New Testaments, when a man wanted to propose to a woman, he had to approach her parents to make a legal, contractual agreement for marriage. It was true of Joseph and Mary in a betrothal period "before they came together" (Matthew 1:18–19). Joseph was Mary's husband-to-be, and Mary would be Joseph's wife. This betrothal time was usually a year (plus or minus a few months) before the actual wedding ceremony. It was a binding agreement, but the couple did not consummate the marriage at that time.

This betrothal time is equivalent to the present "Church Age" here on earth. We, the "Church," are the Bride of Christ. Any repentant sinner who has been born again, baptized by the Holy Spirit, is a member of the "body of Christ" (John 3:3–5; 1 Corinthians 12:13). Christ and His Church are now in a pre-wedding betrothal time before this body of Christ will meet Jesus in the clouds ("The Rapture," 1 Thessalonians 4).

2. The second phase of the marriage custom was for the bridegroom to claim his bride without a day or time announced. His preparation is to make a place for his bride to live in his father's house or build a cottage suitable for the happy couple (John 14:1–3). The best example of this custom was Jesus's statement about the wise and foolish virgins who were waiting for the bridegroom to come for his bride and bring her to his father's house for the wedding ceremony (Matthew 25:1–13). This future event will be the imminent Rapture of the Church to meet Jesus (Bridegroom) in the air and

live in heaven (the Father's house, 1 Thessalonians 4:13–18).

3. The third phase was the preparation of a marriage supper for the guests of the celebration of marriage. This feast and fellowship would last for several days (like the biblical Jewish receptions). We see this illustrated in the wedding at Cana that Jesus and His family lingered to attend (John 2:1–12).[2]

We, as the Church of Jesus Christ, the Bride of Christ, are betrothed to Jesus now on earth. He is in heaven preparing a special place for us as believers, His "wife-to-be." "I go to prepare a place for you, I will come again and receive you to Myself; that where I am, there you may be also" (John 14:2–3).

Christ's Bride Meets Up with the Groom

We, as believers, the children of God, are the Bride of Christ. We all should be watchful for the imminent return of the Bridegroom. It will be the joining of the Bride and the Bridegroom in the clouds for a perfect marriage in heaven (1 Thessalonians 4:13–18). It is comparable to God fashioning the first woman (bride) for Adam and bringing her to him in the garden setting of Eden (Genesis. 2:22). We can imagine a groom standing in front of a church or ceremony stage to meet his bride coming down an aisle to him.

The reception of the grand union is the "Marriage Supper of the Lamb," which will be at the beginning of the millennial reign of Christ (Revelation 19:7, 9). Another prophetic reference of this marriage supper at the time of the Kingdom is Isaiah 25:6–9, which tells of a choice feast with gladness and rejoicing "in His salvation"

(v. 9). Luke 13:29 and 14:15 give great consolation: "Blessed is he who shall (sit down and) eat bread in the kingdom of God!"[3]

Christ's Bride: The Church

We can also see the biblical usage of Christ's Bride in the apostle Paul's doctrine of Christ and His Church. He wrote in two of his epistles that the Church has many members, and he called the Church Christ's "body of believers," collectively as one group (Romans 12 and 1 Corinthians 12). "For as the body is one and has many members, but all the members of that one body, being many, are one body, so also is Christ" (v. 12).

Christ's body of believers is equivalent to His Bride, as the marriage of a husband and wife:

> Husbands, love your wives, just as Christ also loved the Church and gave Himself for her, that He might sanctify and cleanse her with the washing of water by the word, that He might present her to Himself a glorious Church, not having spot or wrinkle or any such thing, but that she should be holy and without blemish. (Ephesians 5:25–27)

The words in this text, "He might present her to Himself a glorious Church," may very well be King Jesus's presentation of His Bride to the world at the beginning of His millennial reign. Then, He will display her to all gathered around His throne at the Marriage Supper of the Lamb. We are His wife, "the Church."

Two other passages use the word "present" as an announcement to Jesus's guests:

> Knowing that He (God) who raised up the Lord Jesus will also raise us up with Jesus and will

present us with you (fellow Corinthian believers).
(2 Corinthians 4:14)

For I am jealous for you … I have betrothed you to
one husband (the Lord Jesus), that I may *present* you
as a chaste virgin to Christ. (2 Corinthians 11:2)

Paul uses the word "chaste" as his motivation that he would prepare the converts to be joined with Christ the Groom as a betrothed, pure bride, ready for her wedding day. The presentation of Christ and His Bride will be as a redeemed, sanctified, and holy Church. They are coupled with Christ and declared to the world as the beauty of Christ's honor and glory.

Christ and the Bride's Reception

We do not see the actual word "bride" in the Ephesians 5 passage, but it is used in Revelation 19:7:

Let us rejoice and be glad and give him glory! For
the wedding of the Lamb has come, and his bride
has made herself ready. (NIV84 and 2011)

Both the New International Versions use the word "bride," and the New King James Version uses "His wife."

"For the marriage of the Lamb has come, and His wife has made herself ready" (v. 7). The best clarification is in Revelation 21:9, which sums up both translations: "Come, I will show you the bride, the Lamb's wife" (NKJV). Both words and descriptions are correct as Jesus will be married to His Bride in heaven after the Rapture.

Revelation 19:11–14 shows that both the Bridegroom and the Bride will be coming to earth on white horses to conquer all evil and enemies of God in the battle of Armageddon (Revelation 16:16).

The "Marriage Supper of the Lamb," after the battle of Armageddon, is Christ's presentation to the world with God's saints and angels (Matthew 25:31). Christ will uniquely make known the glamour, majesty, and beauty of His Bride. More will be stated and explained in the following chapters.

The gathering of the Marriage Supper of the Lamb will be on the earth. It makes sense that when Christ comes to reign on His throne in Jerusalem, the party/reception would be around Zion, where the central activity of events will be to begin His millennial reign. The opening night of this marriage reception of the Bridegroom-King and Bride-wife—there is no mention of a "queen" in the prophetic scheme of things—will identify the preciousness of the "Bride of Christ" as His body of believers. Christ will crown the Church saints with responsibilities in His glorious Millennial Kingdom. In later chapters, we will see that there are duties and responsibilities given to members of Christ's Church.

Christ's Celebration with His Wife

We, as the Church, are waiting for this special day. Revelation 19:5–7 (NIV) urges us to "praise our God."

> Then a voice came from the throne, (possibly an archangel with emphasis), saying: "Praise our God, all you his servants, you who fear him, both great and small!" Then I heard what sounded like a great multitude, like the roar of rushing waters and like loud peals of thunder, shouting: "Hallelujah!" For our Lord God Almighty reigns. Let us be glad and rejoice and give Him glory, for the marriage of the Lamb, has come, and His wife has made herself ready.

In Greek, the meaning of the first phrase is to admonish us to be glad, to rejoice, and to give the Lord glory. The late John F. Walvoord said:

> The verb "praise" is in the present tense and is, therefore, a command to "keep on praising" the Lord their God. The great multitude now announces a major feature of the Lord's reign upon earth, His marriage to His Bride … "Hallelujah" (the fourth time "hallelujah" is used in Revelation 19:5–7).[4]

The Greek then switches from continual praise to a definite "now," that the marriage of the Lamb "has come." (In other words, it is about to happen! It is the time!)

> His bride has made herself ready. Fine linen, bright and clean, was given her to wear. (Revelation 19:7–8 NIV84 and 2011).

In Revelation 21:9, God proclaims, "Come, I will show you the bride, the wife of the Lamb" (NIV84). Are you amazed by all this? There will be a wedding and a reception joining the two together in a Jewish-like ceremony and "marriage feast" for His guests.[5]

Christ Reigning from Zion

Many events will happen in a transition period of judgment coming on the whole earth, before the Marriage Supper of the Lamb, which will be the central focus. Revelation 20 describes who will be at the supper and ushered into the thousand-year kingdom. God will cater and prepare this grand feast for the Bridegroom, who will be seated on His rightful throne:

> Upon the throne of David and over His Kingdom, to order it and establish it with judgment and justice. (Isaiah 9:7)

> Yet I have set My King on My holy hill of Zion. (Psalm 2:6)

He will reign from the city of David, the city of Jerusalem, or "Zion." Joel 3 states that King Jesus will reign from this prophetic city of Zion:

> The Lord also will roar from Zion and utter His voice from Jerusalem … dwelling in Zion my holy mountain. Then Jerusalem shall be holy. (Joel 3:16–17)

This grand city will be the headquarters of King Jesus and "will place salvation in Zion, for Israel My glory" (Isaiah 46:13). There will be rejoicing in Zion in the coming of the Savior King. "Shout, O daughter of Jerusalem! Behold, your King is coming to you; He is just and having salvation" (Zechariah 9:9). The celebration of the Marriage Feast of the Lamb and His inauguration as King on David's throne will be in Jerusalem (Zion).

Christ Has Many Guests

God Himself will set up a stage, Christ's throne. There will be tables to host and feed all the living believers from the seven-year Tribulation still in their bodies of flesh and blood. The godly saints of the Old Testament time and the Tribulation martyrs will be there. Jesus and His Bride, the Church, will be the center of attention. The master of ceremonies will announce the arrival of the Groom and His Bride.

The voice of joy and the voice of gladness, the voice
of the bridegroom and the voice of the bride, the
voice of those who will say: "Praise the LORD of
hosts, for the LORD is good, for His mercy endures
forever—and of those who will bring the sacrifice of
praise into the house of the LORD. For I will cause
the captives of the land to return as at the first," says
the LORD. (Jeremiah 33:11)

What an announcement! All will be joyful, and there will be
singing with comfort in the air all around the guests. This rejoicing
is the "feast of all feasts," which will consummate the wedding. More
of this attendance at the Marriage Supper of the Lamb will be in
chapters 3 and 5 of this book.[6]

Enjoyment and Eating at the Marriage Supper of the Lamb

There will be actual food to eat at this Marriage Feast of the
Lamb. John wrote in Revelation 19:9, "Blessed are those who are
called to the Marriage Supper of the Lamb." Will the glorified
bodies of the saints need food to sustain their bodies? No, not likely.
However, we believe that there will be food.

Christ Ate in His Glorified Body

Jesus was the "first fruit" of those who slept (referring to His
burial in the grave). He is the very first with a glorious, resurrected
body like we will have in the Millennium. After the resurrection,
Jesus ate with His disciples. In the upper room, He asked if they
had any food, and then He ate broiled fish and honeycomb (Luke
24:42). Jesus ate a meal with Cleopas and his companion before He

appeared to the group in the upper room. Luke 24:30, 31 reads: "As He sat at the table with them, He took bread, blessed and broke it, and gave it to them … their eyes were opened, and they knew Him; and He vanished from their sight." How amazing for Cleopas and his friend to walk with Jesus and then hear His teaching around their dining table.

The Lord Jesus in His glorified body also ate with His disciples along the shores of Galilee at a breakfast of roasted fish and bread (John 21:10–14). Food always has a part in Jewish relationships, such as dining with friends. It will be a future festivity of dining with the Lord of lords, our Bridegroom at the Marriage Feast of the Lamb. Therefore, we can imagine that there will be food as well at the future Jewish celebration.

Christ Preincarnate Ate with Abraham

Another biblical illustration of the divine, heavenly beings (similar to our future glorified bodies) dining is when the Lord and two companions appeared to Abraham in Genesis 18:1–33. Abraham knew that they were more than ordinary humans. He commanded his servants to wash their feet, and he asked Sarah to bake bread. He ran to the herd to choose the tender veal cutlets and gave them to the visitors. Abraham "set it all before them and stood by them under the tree as they ate" (Genesis 18: 8).

Biblical scholars who interpret the Genesis 18 meeting with Abraham and the guests believe that this spokesperson was the Lord Jesus Himself. He talked with Abraham about how many righteous men and women would be in Sodom so that He would not destroy that wicked city. The preincarnate Christ Jesus and angels ate what Abraham and Sarah set before them.

Christ Dining with Us

In my forty years in the Philippines, I learned that the Filipino custom is that if visitors come by while you are eating a snack or a meal, you must invite the visitors to eat with you also.

Jesus invites those who are His redeemed people to dine with Him and He with us:

> Behold, I stand at the door and knock. If anyone hears my voice and opens the door, I will come in to him and dine with him, and he with Me. (Revelation 3:20)

The Lord Jesus will prepare His tables of feasting for the Marriage Supper of the Lamb. The whole purpose of the meal is a celebration of our relationship with Him as faithful companions in fellowship with the Bridegroom-King.

Why is it so crucial for us who are living today to anticipate the end-times of a Millennium to come? Some people will ask, "Will we as believers and followers of Christ now see such events as spelled out in the Revelation of Jesus Christ? Would we not just be in heaven with God and not be around on earth as spectators to what will take place?" The Bible is clear as to who will be present and who will be far away from these events—from the judgment they have or will receive. Unbelievers will not be able to see the glamorous episodes as described, but we, as believers, will be there. Continue to read the chapters ahead to find out who will dine with Jesus at the Marriage Supper of the Lamb.

We See Christ Truly as He Is

The Holy Scriptures say that when Jesus returns, "we shall be like Him, for we shall see Him as He is" (1 John 3:2). The Greek

The Glorious Entrance into the Glamorous Kingdom

word used, *homois,* is "to be like, similar, or resemble."[7] We will see Him as He is in all His excellency and honor. God will fulfill all the promises and prophecies in God's revelation of Himself. Even King David truly believed that he would see the Lord's face. Psalm 17:15 says, "As for me, I will see Your face in righteousness; I shall be satisfied when I awake in Your likeness." All of God's believing saints from all ages will be there.[8]

THE PREMILLENIAL REIGN OF CHRIST JESUS THE KING

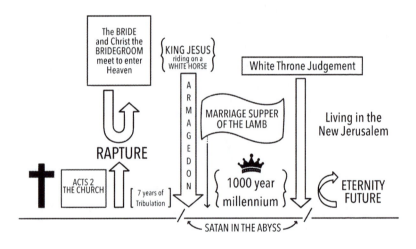

CHAPTER 3

WHO WILL THE GLORIOUS KINGDOM INCLUDE?

I will come again and receive you to Myself;
that where I am, there you may be also.
—John 14:3

The Early Events of the Kingdom and Who Will Be Included

Those whom God has loved and dealt with of all times and ages will be part of these beginning events of Christ's glorious Kingdom. Those who have been in "Abraham's bosom" (Luke 16:22–23, the example of Lazarus), from Adam and Eve to the thief on the cross, will be with Christ in paradise (Luke 23:42–43).

The Glimpse of Paradise

Let us take a moment to talk about the future paradise. Matthew Henry, Dr. Walvoord and Dr. Zuck explain that the ultimate "paradise" is when New Jerusalem is a reality with the "tree of life," yielding its fruit every month (Revelation 21:2 and 22:2).

> To him who overcomes I will give to eat of the tree
> of life, which is in the midst of the Paradise of God.
> (Revelation 2:7)

"Paradise" in Greek, "*paradeisos*," means "a garden or park." The "tree of life" is said to be in the celestial city in the eternal state of New Jerusalem (Revelation 22:2, 14). The excellence of a real "paradise regained" will be after the millennial reign of Christ (as compared to the "paradise lost" that happened in the Garden of Eden).[9]

Furthermore, the thief on the cross would be in this future paradise. Jesus said, "Today you will be with Me in Paradise" (Luke 23:43). The thief was saved that day ("today") at that moment when Jesus was on the cross. He will be included in the Kingdom to come.

The thief said, "Remember me when You come into Your kingdom" (Luke 23:42). He would have read the plaque over Jesus's cross, proclaiming He was the "King of the Jews." Therefore, with all the shouting and ridiculing about being a king, naturally, the thief would say "to remember" him when Jesus would come into His "Kingdom." "Paradise" would be a far cry from the dungeon he had been living in for days or weeks (Luke 23:39–43). Ultimately, for the thief—and for us as saved-from-sin individuals—we will be in the presence of Jesus ("with Me") forever after death. "To be absent from the body and to be present with the Lord" (2 Corinthians 5:8; Philippians 1:23). [10]

Christ's Millennial Kingdom is just a glimpse of what the eternal Garden of Eden will be in the future New Jerusalem (Revelation 21 and 22). The reclamation and remodeling of the earth after the seven-year Tribulation will be just the start of a paradise on earth when Christ returns to rule and reign on His throne in Jerusalem.

King David was envisioning being in Christ's presence in Psalm

23 when he said, "And I will dwell in the house of the LORD forever" (Psalm 23:6). He realized that the Lord was showing him "the path of life; In Your presence is fullness of joy; at Your right hand are pleasures forevermore" (Psalm 16:11).

There are "eternal pleasures" (NIV84) to be near the Savior and at His right hand, even in the millennial reign of Christ. What joy and what anticipation! I get chills just thinking of being at this feast. I want to be near my dear Savior and coming King. How do you feel about the coming King? Are you ready and desiring to be with Him soon?

Christ's promise in John 14:3 is: "Where I am, there you may be also." So, we will be where Jesus is—at the "Marriage Supper of the Lamb." His disciples and beloved ones will be there. Saints of all dispensations will be there for the first evening of the King's coronation.

The Old Testament Saints

The Millennial Kingdom includes three unique groups of saints. There will be faithful believers such as Adam, Noah, Abraham, Moses, David, and the prophets along with the Old Testament saints. They will be resurrected to inherit their tribal destinations in the Messiah's Kingdom for a thousand years. Jesus mentioned a feast that included Abraham, Isaac, and Jacob in the Kingdom. It was demonstrated about these men at a time when Jesus was explaining the faith of the Gentile centurion. He had not found anyone in Israel with "so great a faith" (Matthew 8:10).

Many will be at the Marriage Feast of the Lamb. The previous, present, and even the future saints will be in His millennial reign:

I say to you that many will come from east and the west and will take their place at the feast with

> Abraham, Isaac, and Jacob in the kingdom of
> heaven. (Matthew 8:11 NIV84)

That Roman centurion who believed will be at the inaugural feast. The chosen people of God with Jewish heritage will be there. As well as many other racial born-again believers. Praise be to God who has saved the remnant for His eternal Kingdom Age.

The Tribulation Saints

Secondly, the Tribulation saints will be there:

> And I saw thrones, and they sat on them, and
> judgment was committed to them. Then I saw the
> souls of those who had been beheaded for their
> witness to Jesus and for the word of God, who
> had not worshiped the beast or his image and had
> not received his mark on their foreheads or their
> hands. And they lived and reigned with Christ for
> a thousand years. (Revelation 20:4)

All who have died due to the persecution during the Tribulation will be reigning with Jesus in the Millennium. These saints are those who do not worship the "beast" (the Antichrist).

In the fifth seal, during the Tribulation time, we are told that martyrs are under the altar as the Old Testament priests would slaughter the sacrifices. They were slain because of their preaching and testimony to the Word of God (Revelation 6:9–11). The high-minded politics of the Antichrist will have many Jews, as well as Christians, killed, thinking their God has brought about the tragedies of His wrath poured out on the earth. Unbelievers want to stop God's proclamation because of the conviction laid upon them. They want to purge God's elect from the face of the planet. They express their hostility toward God by killing others who do not favor their satanic influence (Revelation 3:10; 11:10; 13:8; 17:2).

Dr. David Jeremiah's commentary notes state, "These believers will cry out to God, asking Him to render justice for all the devoted who have been murdered during the Tribulation."[11]

They cry out for "justice" in avenging upon their murderers who despitefully use them in a "holocaust" sort of situation during the whole seven-year Tribulation. They are to wait and rest a little longer:

> How long, O Lord, holy and true, until You judge and avenge our blood on those who dwell on the earth?' Then a white robe was given to each of them, and it was said to them that they should rest a little while longer, until both the number of the fellow servants and their brethren, who would be killed as they were, was completed. (Revelation 6:10–11)

These saints will die during the Tribulation and then be glorified to be part of the Millennium to serve King Jesus.

Finally, the judgment of the Judge, King Jesus, will come to pass at the beginning of the Millennium (Matthew 24:9–14; 25:31–32). The wicked will be avenged. The martyred saints will be given thrones. They are to reign with Christ for a thousand years (Revelation 20:4). White garment "robes" will be given to them (6:11). We will learn more about these saints in the chapters to come.

The Church Age Saints

The third group who will be at the Marriage Feast of the Lamb are the Church saints, raptured to meet Jesus in the clouds before the seven-year Tribulation. As explained, a marriage ceremony was sanctioned in heaven when the raptured saints joined up with Christ (1 Thessalonians 4:13–18). The Church is all born-again believers from its beginning in Acts 2 until the Rapture. They are better known or described as the "body of Christ" (1 Corinthians 12:27; Ephesians 4:12).

These "Church saints" are given assurance in Paul's last book (2 Timothy 2:10–12) that they will reign with Christ. These verses connect the end-times with the interpretation of the twenty-four elders mentioned in Revelation 4–5 and Revelation 20:6. These are the priests ruling and reigning with Christ in His Kingdom (Revelation 1:6).

"Priests" in the Bible always represent the mediation between God and men. The Jewish high priest would represent men to God and God to men. The apostle Peter wrote that saints of his time were "a chosen generation, a royal priesthood, a holy nation ... that you (they) may proclaim the praises of Him" (1 Peter 2:9). We, as the Church saints, will be ruling and taking King Jesus's orders and mandates out to the people during the Millennium.

The Excitement of a Wedding Reception

My wife and I have gone to many weddings before and after we were married in the late 1970s. Both she and I were part of the wedding parties of our friends from Bible college. I was even a ring bearer at the age of five for my oldest brother's wedding and an usher in the next two brothers' weddings. My wife and I, to this day, share a few kisses before and after we attend a wedding to show our affection and remembrance of our wedding day and honeymoon.

There is something special about a wedding, whether in a church, garden, or destination location. It is time with friends and family. The marriage feast of Jesus Christ with His Bride will be a splendid occasion.

Everything in this marriage reception with Christ and His coronation as King will be glorious and glamorous in all its splendor and pomp. We, the Bride, are all the New Testament saints from the start of Christ's Church in Acts 2, on the Day of Pentecost to the Rapture of the Church.

What excitement! What more could we ask for then to see Jesus, our Savior and Lord, be praised, honored, and glorified in our midst? We, as members of the body of Christ, the Bride, will have the primary seats next to Jesus on the center throne near all the activity, worship, singing, and praise.

The Events All Happening in the Jerusalem Area

I believe that the transition for events from the victory at the battle of Armageddon, riding the white stallions, and Jesus touching down on the Mount of Olives will happen very quickly (with some devastation along the way in the city of Jerusalem and surrounding Holy Mount suburbs). God will have to make an area for celebration and the reception near or around the actual city of Zion. The old Jerusalem may still stand as a memory, but there will be a New Zion, built up in God's plan and design. Jesus will rightfully take the throne of David! Of course, the capital city of Jerusalem will be the place of His coronation and installation as "King of kings and Lord of lords" (Revelation 19:16).

The Place of the Grand Wedding Reception

Isaiah 25:6 is a prophecy that fits well in the context of the location of the Marriage Supper of the Lamb:

> On this mountain, the LORD Almighty will prepare a feast of rich food for all peoples, a banquet of aged wine—the best of meats and finest wines. (Isaiah 25:6 NIV84)

Isaiah 4:5–6 mentions a glow of God's glory by night and by day. His beauty will shine forth:

> It shall come to pass in that day; that there will be no light; the lights will diminish. It shall be one day, which is known to the LORD —neither day nor night. But at evening time it shall happen; that it will be light. (Zechariah 14:6–7)

Could it be that on that coronation day of Christ and at the approximate time of the Marriage Feast of the Lamb, God will extend light on the evening supper attended by the holy saints and loved ones to be honored?

The Extended Day in the Light of God's Glory

The book of Zechariah repeats the phrase "in that day" that the light of God's glory will extend that celebration into the night hours (Zechariah 14:7). Perhaps Jerusalem will be like the desert wanderings and the Tabernacle years, where the glory of God will be shown with fire by night and a cloud by day. The word "canopy," stated in Isaiah 4:5 (NIV84), could be a divine covering tent, perhaps to continue the festivities of the wedding reception for many days. The expression "in that day of the LORD" (Zechariah 12:8) needs to be considered. There will be so many things happening in Jerusalem at the time Christ begins to reign.

The Example of Glorified Saints

Let us connect what we have learned with a glimpse of the "Mount of Transfiguration" (Matthew 17:1–9). The selected three disciples saw the transfigured Jesus (even before His death and resurrection) with glorified Moses and Elijah. The experience was a token of what it will be like to see the King and Old Testament saints in their glorified bodies. We could conclude this is what the supper gathering will be. Praise the Lord!

The Earth Revitalized and Renewed

At the beginning of the Millennium, there will be a renovation or resurfacing (facelift-renewal) of the earth. It will be necessary because of the turmoil and destruction of the seven-year Tribulation period. The oceans, trees, and vegetation will be a "green earth" again with no human pollution in its waterways. The scriptures say that men will rebuild their homes, condos, villages, and cities again to live peaceably on the earth (Isaiah 61:4).

> "They shall build the waste cities and inhabit them, they shall plant vineyards and drink wine from them. They shall also make gardens and eat fruit from them. I will plant them in their land, and no longer shall they be pulled up from the land I have given them," says the LORD your God. (Amos 9:14–15)

The Millennial Temple will be built on a new site. It will probably be on the north side of the earthquake divide mentioned above (Ezekiel 47:1–3).

All the technology and discoveries men have invented, such as construction equipment (trucks, cranes, payloaders, cement mixers, and steel) will be used to build Christ's temple (Ezekiel 37–39). We read about the detailed dimensions and materials in Ezekiel. Men and women will make a temple compound to worship and give glory and honor to Christ, the Savior and King.

God's Divine Place and Food to Enjoy

Perhaps the decor of the Marriage Supper of the Lamb will be set up by God Himself. He will arrange this reception in and around an area of Jerusalem's suburbs or perhaps a garden somewhere in the Holy Land of Palestine.

Millions of saints will observe and glorify the Lord of lords and King of kings. What a feast of unlimited food and drinks to everyone's content. Perhaps the wine will be likened to what they had in Cana (Christ's first miracle in John 2). There may be specialties of various food dishes from all nations, people, and languages (Daniel 7–12; Revelation 7:9–10). It seems this feast will last for days at the start of the millennial reign of King Jesus.

I conclude from my study that the same earth, moon, and sun we have now will accurately count for a thousand calendar years from the beginning to the end of the Kingdom Age. Since Jesus is the "Alpha and Omega, the Beginning and the End" (Revelation 1:8), all things will be most beautiful, bountiful, and magnificent. There will be prophetic fulfillment to the praise and glory to the Lord God!

Continual Praise and Honor to King Jesus

The millennial rule of Christ will be all to His glory, honor, and majesty. Is it possible that there is a future tense of Psalm 23:5–6?

> You prepare a table before me in the presence of my
> enemies … My cup runs over. Surely goodness and
> mercy shall follow me all the days of my life, and I
> will dwell in the house of the LORD, forever.

King David may have thought of the future enjoyment of being with King Jesus forever and ever. May we all have this expectant hope!

There is a similarity between the "Good Shepherd" in Psalm 23 and the "Great Shepherd" in 1 Peter 5. Born-again believers will indeed be in Zion for the feast of the Lamb. From that supper table, there will be a continuation of dwelling near the presence of the Lord Jesus, the King, forever and forever.

Even now, in our present time, Psalm 23 can be a good reminder that our Good Shepherd can care for you and me. He will look after us even "in the presence of my (our) enemies" (v. 5a). From now on, we have the assurance to dwell with the Lord Jesus forever. We can praise the Lord that God's goodness and mercy will carry us through until the Great and Chief Shepherd shall appear in His greatness and glory (1 Peter 5:4).

Another Feasting in the Valley of Megiddo

During the feasting time in Jerusalem with the Bridegroom-Jesus, we will be around His tables of plenty. Yet, just a few kilometers north, in the Holy Land, there will be vultures and birds of prey. They will be feasting on the dead soldiers' bodies that God had called for their "feast" described in Revelation 19. Christ had just destroyed the enemies with the sword of His mouth. God will call for the vultures, ravens, and beasts for the "supper of the Great God" (Ezekiel 39:17–20). It will be a supper of gorging themselves in the Valley of Megiddo on the bodies of the dead soldiers from the armies of nations that were planning to annihilate Israel (Revelation 19:17–18).

All believers and saints will have the limelight of being in the presence of the Lord Jesus Christ, the Bridegroom, at the "Marriage Supper of the Lamb" (Revelation 19:7–9).

CHAPTER 4

THE FIRST RESURRECTION TO GLORY: THE RAPTURE

Then we who are alive and remain shall be caught up
together with them in the clouds to meet the Lord in
the air. And thus, we shall always be with the Lord.
—1 Thessalonians 4:17

In *Home Alone* (1990), a family was preparing to spend the Christmas holiday in Florida. The family with uncles, aunts, and cousins all got into the special airport shuttle, which took them to the airport, and they boarded the plane. While the jet was taking off, the mother did a head count and realized that their youngest son, Kevin, was not on the airplane. They panicked, but there was nothing they could do. Kevin had the time of his life for the first day or so until he got lonely for his parents and family when Christmas morning came. Kevin's family had flown off in the distance while Kevin was left behind to fend for himself and deal with predators who broke into his family's house. Kevin's loved ones went away and left Kevin behind.

Those Left Behind

Some may remember *A Thief in the Night,* a famous movie from 1972. It had various scenes where the Christians were snatched away by a force or power only possible by God Himself. These Christian believers were taken out from this earth to be seen no more. Their family members, workmates, and neighbors could not find them. "They seemed to vanish into thin air," the loved ones said.

Those "left behind" on earth had to face the hardships of a seven-year Tribulation. Unbelievers were left behind on the earth suddenly, like when a thief breaks in and steals (1 Thessalonian 5:2–4). We know from the New Testament that some will be raptured, and others will be left behind in their homes, workplaces, and communities. A "Left Behind" series of movies, featuring Nicolas Cage, were produced with similar drama. The production studios of Cloud Ten Pictures of St. Catharine's, Ontario, Canada, released the first movies on October 31, 2000, and October 29, 2002.

Many who watched the movie concluded that aliens had taken the vanished people, while the "strong" who remained would have to fend for themselves and make the best of their situation. During those first shocking days, after the people had vanished, some asked for answers from their priests, pastors, or other religious leaders. They even surveyed various churches and found out that the majority of the so-called born-again congregations had disappeared. Literature and Bibles left in people's homes or workplaces were marked by those who had vanished, talking about a future mystery of a "Rapture" to come.

The English word "Rapture" is from the Latin word "*rapturo,*" which means "to be snatched or caught up" (in a Bible context "to the clouds or sky"). All followers of Christ will be raptured to the clouds as Jesus was ascended back to heaven two thousand years ago (Acts 1:9; 1 Thessalonians 4:17). These Christians have believed in the good news of Jesus's finished death on the cross for the forgiveness of their sins.[12]

Spouses or workmates of the raptured Christians may have ignored the witness of those loved ones. Though they had heard of this possible fate, they chose not to believe it. The marked Bibles or pamphlets on the night or coffee tables had these words of the apostle Paul, who wrote this to the Thessalonians:

> But I do not want you to be ignorant, brethren, concerning those who have fallen asleep, lest you sorrow as others who have no hope. For if we believe that Jesus died and rose again, even so, God will bring with Him those who sleep in Jesus. For this, we say to you by the word of the Lord, that we who are alive and remain until the coming of the Lord (Jesus) will by no means precede those who are asleep. For the Lord, Himself will descend from heaven with a shout, with the voice of an archangel, and with the trumpet of God. And the dead in Christ will rise first. Then we who are alive (as believers) and remain shall be caught up together with them in the clouds to meet the Lord in the air. And thus, we shall always be with the Lord. Therefore comfort one another with these words. (1 Thessalonians 4:13–18)

Those Who Vanish into Thin Air

First Thessalonians 4:13–18 is the primary text for this future imminent return of Jesus Christ. Those who will vanish will be taken up to the clouds to meet Jesus in the clouds before being transported to heaven. The unbelievers will be left behind on earth. They will view the crisis as if these loved ones or neighbors just "vanished into thin air."

The message of the passage is for followers of Jesus not to worry about their parents or relatives who have died in Christ. They have a secure hope for a future home in heaven with Jesus. These snatched believing saints in the Rapture will also have a future to be with Christ in the second phase of His revelation before He sets up His Millennial Kingdom on the earth.

Did you notice in verse 16, those who are dead in the graves and know Jesus as their Savior are asleep bodily (their souls being with the Lord in heaven) in the cemeteries until Christ comes down to the clouds to raise up their bodies? There will be the sound of the trumpet, and the archangel will shout to raise those dead bodies (v. 16). They will be resurrected into glorified bodies to be with God high above the atmosphere in His heaven. Those who are alive at the Rapture will be caught up together with Christ in the clouds to be forever with Him in heaven.

The Believer's Soul Rising to Heaven

The apostle Paul also wrote about death and separation for a time from loved ones in 2 Corinthians 5:8, which says that true believers are "absent from the body, present with the Lord." The soul of a Christian will someday leave its body to be in the presence of his or her Lord. Isn't that a reassuring verse for the time of death? It makes us just want to praise the Almighty God much more. God is worthy of our praise and adoration! In these verses, God has revealed to His apostles to write it all down so that we, in this present age, may not be ignorant of these very grand revelations of times to come (1 Thessalonians 4:13–18).

A Resurrection to New Life

There is a resurrection of His saints to come. The Old Testament scriptures speak of a future "resurrection." Martha, the devoted sister of Mary and Lazarus, mentioned in John 11 that she knew of a "resurrection" to come. But Jesus wanted to impress on her and others who were mourning for the death of Lazarus that He is the true and living "Resurrection."

> He said, "I am the resurrection and the life ... Do you believe this?" (John 11:25–26)

He will give the resurrection power to all who believe. He showed to the audience at the grave of Lazarus that He could raise the dead.

He rose from the grave on the Sunday after His cruel crucifixion. He is the first of those resurrected who did not die again. Those who Jesus and the prophets resurrected from the dead finally died again. Jesus, the Savior and Lord will die no more! He is the Living Savior and Redeemer for all those who believe His payment of death and power to resurrect as He had promised. How about you? Do you know in your heart that the glorified Jesus is resurrected from the grave? Do you believe that you will be resurrected and glorified to live with Him forever? You can know this for sure. Please keep reading on about the glorious resurrection message the Bible has for all of us who believe. Yes, we can say, "Praise the Lord!"

Faith Is Not in Vain

The apostle Paul reemphasized the importance of the "Resurrection" in 1 Corinthians 15:

> Now if Christ is preached that He has been raised from the dead, how do some among you say that there is no resurrection of the dead? But if there is no resurrection of the dead, then Christ is not risen. And if Christ is not risen, then our preaching is empty and your faith is also empty. Yes, and we

are found false witnesses of God, because we have testified of God that He raised up Christ, whom He did not raise up—if in fact the dead do not rise. For if the dead do not rise, then Christ is not risen. And if Christ is not risen, your faith is futile; you are still in your sins! Then also those who have fallen asleep in Christ have perished. If in this life only we have hope in Christ, we are of all men the most pitiable. But now Christ is risen from the dead, and has become the firstfruits of those who have fallen asleep. For since by man came death, by Man also came the resurrection of the dead. For as in Adam all die, even so in Christ all shall be made alive. But each one in his own order: Christ the firstfruits, afterward those who are Christ's at His coming. (1 Corinthians 15:12–23)

Are you getting the gist of how Paul has been reasoning with the believers in Corinth? Do you see that all the time, Paul taught, —and the Corinthians believed in—a resurrection to come? Christ Jesus is the "firstfruits" of those who sleep. The "firstfruits" is the first picking of the fruit from the orchards or the first bushel of grain from the fields of harvest (Exodus 23:19; Deuteronomy 18:4). Jesus is the "first" of the glorious, resurrected bodies. And we too, as Christians, will have a new body like His before being ushered into His Kingdom.

Let us see more of what the apostle Paul said about bodies buried and resurrected in a transformation that is glorious and ready when Jesus returns to set up His Kingdom.

But someone will say, "How are the dead raised? And with what body do they come?" Foolish one, what you sow is not made alive unless it dies. And what you sow, you do not sow that body that shall be, but mere grain—perhaps wheat or some other grain. But God gives it a body as He pleases, and to each seed its own body. All flesh is not the same flesh, but there is one kind of flesh of men, another flesh of animals ... there are also celestial bodies and terrestrial bodies ... so also is the resurrection of the dead. The body (man's flesh) is sown in corruption, it is raised in incorruption. It is sown in dishonor; it is raised in glory. It is sown in weakness, it is raised in power. It is sown a natural body, it is raised a spiritual body. (1 Corinthians 15:35–44).

I grew up on a farm where we planted tall yellow field corn that we fed to the dairy cows. We sold the milk to make our daily living. My dad, my brothers, and our neighbors prepared fertile soil for planting the corn seed each spring. I remember one of the men would purchase the hybrid corn seed at the farmers' feed store. They would also buy fertilizer to be planted with the corn seeds. As a boy, I watched the planting process.

At that time, our farm only had a mechanized two-row corn planter that made a furrow to drop the corn seed in with a little fertilizer on top. A final wheel covered everything up in the cornrows. That was in the late 1950s. The men bought a four-row corn planter in the 1960s, a six-row planter in the 1970s, and an eight-row planter later. Now, in the twenty-first century, highly technological large farms have ten- to twelve-row planters for corn, soybeans, peas, or string beans, in long uniformed rows on acres of cultivated, prepared farmland. In all this process of planting, the farmer wants to use the best seeds.

A few years ago, I heard of some farmers who mortgaged their house or property to plant more than two hundred thousand dollars of corn seed with fertilizer in their fields for a six-month harvest. Of course, they paid off their mortgage as soon as the funds came in from the yield. That is trusting God and doing big business!

A Seed Grows up to New Life

As you read from the scriptures and know something about agriculture, a seed must be planted and buried to spring up to glorious life for a harvest. Burying the seeds is the only way to get an eventual profit and higher payback. God intends that His followers someday will die and be buried so that something glorious would happen. We will be resurrected to a new life and preparation for a new realm. Max Lucado said, "The cemetery is not a resting place, but rather the transformation place."[13] How true!

For your continual study, please read and meditate on 1 Corinthians 15. The verses explain that we who are in Christ will have a glorified bodily change, just as Jesus had after His resurrection. We, in our perishable bodies, will be changed into imperishable, immortal beings. God intended for us to live with Him. God, who is eternal, and we, with Christ, will live forever:

> It is sown in dishonor, it is raised in glory. It is sown in weakness, it is raised in power. It is sown a natural body, it is raised a spiritual body. There is a natural body, and there is a spiritual body. And so it is written, "The first man Adam became a living being." (1 Corinthians 15:43, 44; Genesis 2:7)

> The last Adam became a life-giving spirit. However, the spiritual is not first, but the natural, and afterward the spiritual. The first man was of the earth, made of dust; the second Man is the Lord from heaven. As was the man of dust, so also are those who are made of dust; and as is the heavenly Man, so also are those who are heavenly. And as we have borne the image of the man of dust, we shall also bear the image of the heavenly Man. Now, this I say, brethren, that flesh and blood cannot

inherit the kingdom of God; nor does corruption inherit incorruption. Behold, I tell you a mystery: We shall not all sleep, but we shall all be changed— in a moment, in the twinkling of an eye, at the last trumpet. For the trumpet will sound, and the dead will be raised incorruptible, and we shall be changed. For this corruptible must put on incorruption, and this mortal must put on immortality. So when this corruptible has put on incorruption, and this mortal has put on immortality, then shall be brought to pass the saying that is written: "Death is swallowed up in victory." (1 Corinthians 15:45–54, Isaiah 25:8)

Our Mortality Turning to an Immortal Body

It is exciting to read these verses. Paul uses parallels from earthly, farming realities to describe a transformation of a "resurrection of these mortal bodies" to a glorious immortal body. It will be worth it all in a victorious transfer from earth to *glory*.

How do you feel about a resurrection to glory? Where do you fit into this picture of being translated? Do you look forward to being transformed into something greater on that day when Christ comes and we are snatched away in the Rapture?

Will Christ claim you for that "Resurrection Day" to be promoted to reign in His glorious Kingdom? These are questions we need to answer for ourselves with God. May God bless us all and those who have gone before us in the ground to wait until that grand day chosen for us, His saints.

CHAPTER 5

THE GLORIOUS CLOTHING PREPARED FOR THE MARRIAGE FEAST

Blessed are those who are called to the
Marriage Supper of the Lamb!
—Revelation 19:9

Revelation 20:6 tells that those who take part in the Rapture ("First Resurrection") are "blessed and holy." They are ready to be revealed with Christ at the Marriage Feast of the Lamb. Read this verse with intent:

Blessed and holy is he who has part in the first resurrection! Over such the second death has no power, but they will be priests of God and of Christ, and shall reign with Him a thousand years. (Revelation 20:6)

Earlier, I mentioned that people all over the world enjoy weddings. Parents and participants pray that the marriage will continue by God's grace in love and harmony for a lifetime to come. With a wedding ceremony comes a reception or feast. (In the Philippines, the groom pays for the wedding reception. In the United States, the bride's parents' foot the bill). At the Marriage Feast of the Lamb, the "father of the groom" (our heavenly Father) puts on the "feast." The announcement of the celebration comes from the throne of heaven. (Revelation 19:1–7).

The Proper Clothes to Attend

In Matthew 22, Jesus told a parable that may reveal the thought behind the scenes for the final days before the Millennial Kingdom. It speaks of a wedding feast given and presented to exalt our Savior, Jesus Christ. The host invites guests who would be obliged to come. Matthew 22:1–14 helps explain some parallels of similarity, which may be in store for the kingdom coronation:

> And Jesus answered and spoke to them again by parables and said: "The kingdom of heaven is like a certain king who arranged a marriage for his son, and sent out his servants to call those who were invited to the wedding; and they were not willing to come." Again, he sent out other servants, saying, "Tell those who are invited, See, I have prepared my dinner; my oxen and fatted cattle are killed, and all things are ready. Come to the wedding.'" But they made light of it and went their ways, one to his own farm, another to his business. And the rest seized his servants, treated them spitefully, and killed them. But when the king heard about it, he was furious. And he sent out his armies, destroyed those murderers, and burned up their city. Then he said to his servants, "The wedding is ready, but those who were invited were not worthy. Therefore go into the highways, and as many as you find, invite

to the wedding." So those servants went out into the highways and gathered together all whom they found, both bad and good. And the wedding hall was filled with guests. But when the king came in to see the guests, he saw a man there who did not have on a wedding garment. So he said to him, "Friend, how did you come in here without a wedding garment?" And he was speechless. Then the king said to the servants, "Bind him hand and foot, take him away, and cast him into outer darkness; there will be weeping and gnashing of teeth. For many are called, but few are chosen." (Matthew 22:1–14)

This story gives some heavenly meaning and interpretation for those invited to Christ's inaugural feast. Who are these extra guests invited to the Marriage Feast of the Lamb? Some commentators say that God has offered His invitation to His Jewish people, but they have rejected Him and His wishes for them.

Since the Jews did not come to Him willingly, He offered the invitation to all people that "whosoever will, may come" (John 3:16; 2 Corinthians 5:14–15; 1 Timothy 2:6; 4:10; Titus 2:11; Hebrews 2:9). The servants had gone out to invite many more from pagan backgrounds and Gentiles. God wants to open a broader spectrum of those saved by grace. He wants to give them wedding garments appropriate to attend the marriage feast. We all can praise the Lord for His great love for humanity "that He gave His only begotten Son, that whoever believes on Him should not perish, but have everlasting life" (John 3:16).

Those who reject God's offer of salvation will have judgment awaiting them. God, through His Son Jesus, will judge with destruction and annihilation during the time of the seven-year Tribulation and the battle of Armageddon. Judgment from King Jesus will come before any kind of celebration begins His millennial reign. The unbelievers have rejected what God has prepared—even though God made a sacrificial payment for them to attend this future feast. Sadly, many of the invited do not get on board, and then it is too late to take part.

Praise God! There is an invitation for you to the King's feast for His Son. I hope you will be there with the right wedding garments. Will you accept Christ as your sin substitute and be a guest—or will you reject His invitation?

Rejection for Those Not in the Proper Attire

The story continues with the king finding someone not wearing the proper wedding attire. That person was rejected and cast out for eternal punishment, not to be allowed to return. What a terrible fate for the one who thought the invitation was open to anyone but was not issued the correct garments to wear for the marriage feast. However, since the invitation was open to all to come and not the selected ones only—some accepting and some refusing the king's request—some got into the feast without the proper attire. The man without the proper wedding attire stood out from the rest. There was a quick rejection from attending the marriage feast. (A note of clarification: Not all parables of Jesus have every detail a direct carryover to the actual future prophecy). All who are Jesus's own reconciled believers will have the proper radiant white elegant linen attire for the Marriage Supper of the Lamb.

Jesus mentioned a casting out of some from the feast (the Marriage Supper of the Lamb) in His early ministry. When Jesus had a conversation about the "great faith" of the Roman centurion, He said that the centurion would be with Abraham, Isaac, and Jacob at the "feast." Others would be rejected:

> But the sons of the kingdom will be cast out into outer darkness. There will be weeping and gnashing of teeth. (Matthew 8:12)

Christ Abiding in the Believer

So, what would have happened to the Gentile guests who were along the highway and hedges and received the correct garments to wear? Here is the scriptural proof for the appropriate clothing and ways to be accepted by the Lord:

> I will greatly rejoice in the LORD; my soul shall be joyful in my God; for He has clothed me with the garments of salvation, He has covered me with the robe of righteousness. (Isaiah 61:10)

> Rather, clothe yourselves with the Lord Jesus Christ, and do not think about how to gratify the desires of the sinful nature. (Romans 13:14 NIV84)

Note: Other translations interpret "clothe" as to "'put on" the Lord Jesus Christ, and make no provision for the flesh, "to fulfill its lust" (NKJV).[14]

> Therefore, if anyone is in Christ, he is a new creation; old things have passed away, behold, all things have become new. (2 Corinthians 5:17)

> There is therefore now no condemnation to those who are in Christ Jesus. (Romans 8:1)

> And now, little children, abide in Him, that when He appears, we may have confidence and not be ashamed before Him at His coming. (1 John 2:28)

> To them, God willed to make known what are the riches of the glory of this mystery among the

Gentiles: which is Christ in you, the hope of glory.
(Colossians 1:27)

Do you see how an outsider (Gentile) needed to be clothed with preparation for the Marriage Feast of the Lamb? The logical answer is all need to be in Jesus Christ Himself. We were placed "in Christ" at the time of our salvation. At that moment, God truly saved us from our sins, and He rightfully invited us to His inaugural "reception." This spectacular event will be the "hope of glory" (Titus 2:13). We will be included in the Marriage Feast of the Lamb in the Millennial Kingdom.

The Purity of the Correct Apparel

In Revelation 7:9,13–14, John the apostle writes of the New Testament Church saints. They will wear garments of white. White has always been a symbol of purity or sanctification. In biblical times, Jewish garments were washed in a bleach substance that took out any kind of impurities, stains, or the natural color of the wool or flax threads. Dirt, soil, and grease are opposite to the purity of being thoroughly clean and white. Cleansing of cloth material is necessary. Similarly, any stain of sin must be purged pure white by God for us to be clothed in His righteousness.

The doctrine of substitutionary atonement is the belief that Christ died in our place, as a substitute for our sins (2 Corinthians 5:21). Second Corinthians 5:1–8 talks about being "clothed." The context is when we pass from this earth in death. The scriptures say, "We earnestly desire to be clothed with our habitation which is from heaven" (v. 2). Mortality must be "reckoned with" for the future spiritual body to be present with the Lord (vv. 3–8). This passage, coupled with Romans 5:17–21, has the saved believer reconciled with the "gift of righteousness" (v. 17). Many theologians say that "we who are sons of God" are clothed in His "righteousness to life eternal" (5:21).

Revelation 3:4–5 speaks of "white clothing" as the garments that God gives the true ones of His. Jesus is speaking to these saints who have been loyal to Him:

> You have a few names even in Sardis who have not defiled their garments; and they shall walk with Me in white, for they are worthy. He who overcomes shall be clothed in white garments, and I will not blot out his name from the Book of Life; but I will confess his name before My Father and before His angels.

The Church as the Twenty-four Elders

Revelation 4 mentions the garments of the twenty-four elders who represent the Church saints.

> Around the throne were twenty-four thrones, and on the thrones, I saw twenty-four elders sitting, clothed in white robes; and they had crowns of gold on their heads … The twenty-four elders fall down before Him (Jesus) who sits on the throne and worship Him who lives forever and ever and cast their crowns before the throne. (Revelation 4:4,10)

When Jesus is riding the white stallion, there will be accompanying Him those from heaven who will be riding white horses also. These could very well be the Church saints as described from these earlier verses or angels coming to judge and make war against the evil enemies.

Some believe Jesus's companions on white horses are angels, but why would angels need horses?

> And the armies in heaven, clothed in fine linen, white and clean, followed Him on white horses. (Revelation 19:14)

In Revelation 3, honor was given to "overcomers" as being "watchful" at the church in Sardis (v. 3). "They are worthy" (v. 4). Also, these verses reveal that all of God's beloved born-again Christ-followers will be walking with Him in garments of "white" (vv. 4–5).

Matthew Henry states, "In the stola, the white robes of justification, and adoption, and honour and glory in the other world. The purity of grace shall be rewarded with the perfect purity of glory."[15]

A "stola" was a long garment, descending to the ankles made of linen; usually worn by Roman women (*Merriam-Webster*).[16] Other research mentions "stola" as a tunic or toga sort of garment for men and women.

Throughout the book of Revelation, the glorified saints are "dressed in white" (3:5; 4:4 NIV) or "clothed in (or with) white robes" (Revelation 4:4; 7:9 NKJV).

> Let us be glad and rejoice and give Him glory, for the marriage of the Lamb has come, and His wife has made herself ready. And to her it was granted to be arrayed in fine linen, clean and bright, for the fine linen is the righteous acts of the saints. (Revelation 19:7–8)

As the glorified "Bride of Christ" or Christ's "wife," the Church will be dressed in white "fine linen" coming on white horses behind or beside the conquering King Jesus (Revelation 19:14–16). Later, when further judgment is complete, all will be attending the

"Marriage Supper of the Lamb" dressed in fine linen (Revelation 19:7–9, 14–16).

These Church saints "are the ones who come out of the Great Tribulation, and washed their robes and made them white in the blood of the Lamb" (Revelation 7:14). They are the ones in the "fine white linen," riding on the white horses to attend the Marriage Supper of the Lamb. They will rule and reign with Jesus Christ the conquering King (2 Timothy 2:12; Revelation 19:16). All born-again believers as Christians in the Church Age will have these dynamic events taken place to live with God's only begotten Son forever (John 3:16).

The Ticket for Heaven

In conclusion, those in the Millennial Kingdom can only be the ones God has saved by His grace alone. According to Ephesians 2:8–9, we cannot say we have gained any merit of good deeds to favor the salvation God has granted us. When God saves us from our sin and the penalty, He makes us a part of Christ, and Christ is in us by His Spirit —the Holy Spirit who dwells in all who are in Christ.

> But you are not in the flesh but the Spirit, if indeed the Spirit of God dwells in you. Now if anyone does not have the Spirit of Christ, he is not His. And if Christ is in you, the body is dead because of sin, but the Spirit is life because of righteousness. But if the Spirit of Him who raised Jesus from the dead dwells in you, He who raised Christ from the dead will also give life to your mortal bodies through His Spirit who dwells in you. (Romans 8:9–11)

I often ask my students at the Bible college, "What is the ticket that allows us to get to heaven when we die or at the Rapture?" I ask you now, as my readers, is it faith? Is it doing good works? Is it being confirmed or baptized? Is it receiving Jesus Christ? The answer is this: The Holy Spirit dwelling in us whom God has given at our salvation. If we are not in Christ, and His Spirit is not abiding in our hearts and lives, there is no way we will get to heaven or be clothed with the wardrobe of His righteousness. Nor will we be included in the Marriage Feast of the Lamb. The ticket for heaven is the Holy Spirit that God has given us at our born-again experience. Anyone can say they are a Christian and not be on their way to heaven. God seals us with the Holy Spirit at the moment of our salvation, as the scripture has promised (Ephesians 1:13).

An Example of Genesis 3

God clothed Adam and Eve after they sinned in the Garden of Eden. God made them tunics (or clothing) from the skins of the sacrificial sheep. The sheep lost their lives to make Adam and Eve the clothes as the substitute for disobedience. It cleared up their matter of sin and resulted in a right relationship with their Maker, God (Genesis 3:21).

Just like God gave the sacrifice of the life of the sheep for the first couple; God gave the sacrifice of Jesus Christ's life up for our sins. What a testimony of God's love for us and the salvation He has freely given. Salvation is all of God. If someone says, "I have a strong faith," "I believe in Jesus," or "I received Him as a child, have been confirmed, or even baptized," it seems that their trust is a very "I-centered," human, personified answer. Instead, we should say, "God has saved me from my sins," and His "Spirit bears witness with our spirit that we are children of God" (Romans 8:16). Amen!

CHAPTER 6

CHRIST'S GLORY DISRUPTED BY IMPOSTERS

I am the LORD, that is My name, and My
glory I will not give to another.
—Isaiah 42:8

Jesus told many stories, preaching, and parables to prepare people for the Millennial Kingdom. He warned masters and their stewards to be ready when their landlord would return. If they had been faithful, he would give them more responsibilities.

Jesus said to his disciples and others around him, "Occupy until I come" (Luke 19:13 KJV). The newer translations say, "Do business till I come" (NKJV) or "Put this money to work ...until I come back" (19:13 NIV84). Consequently, we are to make "business" until Jesus returns in the "revelation" of Himself for His Second Advent to reign in His Kingdom. Yes, we all need to be busy about the Lord's work and mission now to be good stewards of the gifts and talents He has given us.

The true treasures we have are stored up in heaven for a reward (even crowns) and greater responsibility designated for use in the future (Matthew 6:20–21). At the same time, we should beware about the future of false "christs" or false prophets, who would deceive us and the whole world. Imposters of the true and living

Christ Jesus will be invading our lives, loyalty, and liability. Who should we give our allegiance to? Only Christ Jesus, our Savior and Lord.

The Deception Coming by Many Imposters of the Faith

Jesus Himself said on His Mount Olivet discourse before His cruel death on the cross, "Beware!" and look out for imposters.

> Then if anyone says to you, "Look, here is the Christ!" or "There," do not believe it. For false christs and false prophets will rise and show great signs and wonders to deceive, if possible, even the elect. See, I have told you beforehand. (Matthew 24:23ff)

The warning was given many years ago for believers and nonbelievers to be wary of falsehoods. Men will dress up like wolves in sheep's clothing (tyrants who want to deceive people).

> Beware of false prophets, who come to you in sheep's clothing, but inwardly they are ravenous wolves. (Matthew 7:15)

The Coming of the Evil Antichrist

Matthew 24 says that there will be a wicked man. He is a regular man with flesh and blood. However, he will possibly be protected by Satan's forces and empowered to be a leader with prestige. He will desecrate the Jerusalem Temple with a sacrifice that brings "abomination of desecration" to God's holy person (v. 15). We see this in both the book of Revelation and in Daniel. This evil man is the Antichrist, who will, at first, be kind and make peace treaties during the Tribulation period. He breaks the agreements at the halfway point of the Tribulation. Portrayed as "Jacob's troubles" (Jeremiah 30:7), the last three and half years of the Tribulation are turbulent for the Jewish people around the world, especially in Israel (Daniel 11:16, 41).

In Christ's Mount Olivet discourse (Matthew 24, 25), Jesus reveals that the Antichrist goes into the Temple of Jerusalem to desecrate it. The atrocity will be a sacrilegious sacrifice of some kind that will be a terrible offense to the Jewish priests and, of course, to the holy character of God. The Antichrist may even set himself up as the savior. He will be so full of ideas, plans, and leadership skills that many will believe him. He will be "the answer" or "savior" for the world's problems like uprisings, terror attacks, and religious hierarchy.

It says in Daniel that this Antichrist will speak pompous words, which many will believe. It will consequently give him power and authority.

> I was considering the horns (of the fourth beast), and there was another horn, a little one, coming up among them, before whom three of the first horns were plucked out by the roots. And there, in this horn (the Antichrist), were eyes like the eyes of a man, and a mouth speaking pompous words … I watched then because of the sound of the pompous words which the horn was speaking; I watched till the beast was slain, and its body destroyed and given to the burning flame. (Daniel 7:8, 11)

This terrifying world leader (the Antichrist is also known as "this little horn") comes to great power and might have boastful words that appeal to many around the world. He will have a following to solve many problem areas around the political world.

Another prophetic verse, Daniel 9:27, points out the clever way that this Antichrist will make a covenant with Israel and other treaties for peace. Later, in the middle of the seven-year Tribulation, he will break the covenant to make a dreadful "abomination of desolation."

> Then he shall confirm a covenant with many for one week (representing seven years in Daniel's seventh-week prophecy), but in the middle of the week, he shall bring an end to sacrifice and offering. And on the wing of abominations shall be one who makes desolate, even until the consummation, which is determined, is poured out on the desolate. (Daniel 9:27)

These Bible references match many things happening in Revelation 12:13–14 and Revelation 13:5. Satan has and will influence and empower these imposters "big time" during these last weeks of the later half of the seven-year Tribulation. There will be an event where Satan will be cast out of heaven, knowing his time will be shortened before he will be sent to the "abyss" to be chained up during the millennial reign of Christ (Revelation 20:1–3).

The Coming of the Dragon

This "evil one" is described as that "old serpent" or "the dragon."

> The great dragon ... called the devil and Satan, who deceives the whole world with his angels (demons). (Revelation 12:9–14)

Satan and his crew of demons will persecute the people of Israel, God's chosen people, called "the woman who gave birth to the male child" (Jesus).

> Now when the dragon saw that he had been cast to the earth, he persecuted the woman who gave birth to the male Child. But the woman was given two wings of a great eagle, that she might fly into the wilderness to her place, where she is nourished for a time and times and half a time, from the presence of the serpent. (Revelation 12:13–14)

In this context, we see that Satan had a conflict with Michael, the archangel. Michael prevailed over Satan, the old dragon. The devil and his demons made havoc with the people of the earth (v. 12). Satan especially persecuted the Jewish race, and they had to flee to the desert to be cared for by the Lord God (v. 14). This was during the last half of the seven-year Tribulation.

The mid-Tribulation time that the deception of Satan and the Antichrist will be fierce for three and a half years. A "time" is one year, the "times" is two years in addition to the "half time" adds up to the three and a half years remaining until Christ comes in victory to set up His Kingdom. Yes, Jesus will conquer, but that second half of the Great Tribulation will be devastating to the Jewish people and the glorious land of Palestine. In Daniel's prophecy, Jesus described the place of the outrage during the "Great Tribulation" (Matthew 24:15, 21).

> He shall speak pompous words against the Most High. He shall persecute the saints of the Most High and shall intend to change times and law. Then the saints shall be given into his hand for a time and times and half a time. (Daniel 7:25)

> Then I heard the man (the Son of God) clothed
> in linen, who was above the waters of the river,
> when he held up his right hand and his left hand
> to heaven and swore by Him who lives forever,
> that it shall be for a time, times, and half a time;
> and when the power of the holy people (Israel) has
> been completely shattered, all these things shall be
> finished. (Daniel 12:7)

The Coming of the Signs and False Prophets

As we continue with Jesus's teaching in Matthew 24, there are
warning signs that will depict the last days before Christ comes back:

> And you will hear of wars and rumors of wars. See
> that you are not troubled; for all these things must
> come to pass, but the end is not yet. For nation
> will rise against nation, and kingdom against
> kingdom. And there will be famines, pestilences,
> and earthquakes in various places. All these are the
> beginning of sorrows. Then they will deliver you up
> to tribulation and kill you, and you will be hated by
> all nations for My name's sake. And then many will
> be offended, will betray one another, and will hate
> one another. Then many false prophets will rise up
> and deceive many. (Matthew 24:6–11)

Many religious and political deceivers will come. Some will say,
"I am the Christ," but they are imposters and are not the real Lord
Jesus Christ. Daniel spoke of the Antichrist and his "abomination of
desolation." We see the way fake news has brought about imposters
who are contrary to the principles of God's Word, the Bible. Many
twist words to fit certain agendas and platforms for people to believe

and follow. Imposters use social media for their propaganda in fostering many "antichrists" (Matthew 24:24). Jesus also describes the end-times in this fashion in Matthew 24:15ff

> Therefore, when you see the "abomination of desolation," spoken of by Daniel the prophet, standing in the holy place (whoever reads, let him understand), "Then let those who are in Judea flee to the mountains. Let him who is on the housetop not go down to take anything out of his house. And let him who is in the field not go back to get his clothes. But woe to those who are pregnant and to those who are nursing babies in those days! And pray that your flight may not be in winter or on the Sabbath. For then there will be Great Tribulation, such as has not been since the beginning of the world until this time, no, nor ever shall be. And unless those days were shortened, no flesh would be saved; but for the elect's sake those days will be shortened." (Matthew 24:15–22)

In conclusion, all these signs and the dominance of Satan's wrath against the children of Israel point to the soon coming of Jesus Christ to make things right. He will judge the deceivers and impostors to put an end to their difficulties as He sets up His glorious Millennial Kingdom. Victory is in sight for all who will trust Christ to the end (Revelation 5:5–6).

The Deceptiveness of the Tribulation Time of Troubles

The troubles and tribulations of the end-times before the Second Coming of Christ as King for His millennial reign will be treacherous. People on the earth during the seven-year Tribulation period will go through both God's wrath and Satan's fiery trials (Revelation 14:12; 15:1, 7; 16:19).

The Coming of Many Persecutions

This is the beginning of sorrows and persecutions for the Jewish people in their promised land of Palestine. The desertion of running to the hills will not be only occasionally, but many times, because of the troublesome times known as "Jacob's troubles" (Jeremiah 30:7). There will be an escalation of persecutions from the beastly demands and persuasion against God's people, Israel. Christians will want to pray more for the "peace of Jerusalem" (Psalm 122:6–7). "All these are the beginning of sorrows" (Matthew 24:8).

The Lord God will save and help in these troublesome times. There will be ridicule and pressures of persecution—as at the time of Adolf Hitler of Germany. He killed six million Jews during WWII. If people hide during this seven-year Tribulation time or are fortunate to still be alive with the salvation of a born-again Christian experience, which comes through the preaching of the Gospel, they will be saved to go into Christ's Millennial Kingdom. How blessed is the Lord our God who will protect His beloved Jews and Christians alike to help them endure to the end?

The Coming of the 144,000

God, in His providence and grace, will set a seal on the forehead of God's chosen people (Revelation 7:1–8). The Lord God wants to protect twelve thousand Jewish descendants from each one of the twelve sons of Jacob (a total of 144,000). The context of these verses is a special "seal" for the 144,000 Jews (Revelation 7:2, 4). They have a seal that will be a protection over them, which is different than the "mark of the beast" (Revelation 13:18; 20:4). These 144,000 witnesses from various countries around the world, will be God's spokespeople during the seven-year Tribulation. Jesus made it clear that He will call many (both Jews and Gentiles) to preach the "Gospel of the kingdom" (Matthew 24:14). There will be no better time than in the Tribulation to preach the "Kingdom" since Christ's coming will be very near. God will still be working through the Holy Spirit with those who are ready for God's salvation. "Faith comes by hearing ... the Word of God" (Romans 10:17). The message of God's good news, the Gospel, will be carried forth even in difficult times (Acts 1:8).

Therefore, these witnesses of the Gospel will continue in the troublesome Tribulation. They will tell the same message of Jesus and be saved through the same grace given by God (Ephesians 2:8–9). All people of the world need a Redeemer for the salvation of their souls. Have you had that salvation experience?

The Coming of the Two Witnesses

As time passes, two of those persecuted during the Tribulation are witnesses who will be put to death (Revelation 11:3–10). The world, because of their blindness to God, will reject those two special witnesses. The two preachers will speak the truth, yet as time will tell, they will be killed and left lying in the streets. The people of Jerusalem, having been already satanically influenced and indifferent, will leave those two witnesses dead in the streets of "the great city." Most commentators believe that the media will view these two dead bodies for three and a half days in Jerusalem (v. 8). According to Revelation 11:9, the city officials will not allow them to be buried in decent graves.

Revelation 11:10 states that many people of the earth will see this event and rejoice. Emotions are stirred up. One translation says that every tongue, tribe, and nation will "make merry." Gifts will be given "to one another" (v. 10). They will be merry and celebrate that those two witnesses are killed as their bodies just rot in the streets. While the cameras record those watching up close, with some staying back due to the smell of their rotting corpses, they will come to life again in the middle of the fourth day. They will stand on their feet, and a voice from heaven will say, "Come up here" (v. 12).

The scriptures explain what happens and the amazement of the world as they watch this happen on the media:

> And they heard a loud voice from heaven saying to them, "Come up here." And they ascended to heaven in a cloud, and their enemies saw them. At the same hour, there was a great earthquake, and a tenth of the city fell. In the earthquake, seven thousand people were killed, and the rest were afraid and gave glory to the God of heaven. (Revelation 11:12–13)

What a sight! What glory God will proclaim to the world about His preachers of the Gospel.

After the resurrection of these two witnesses, many will remember the amazing, holy miraculous works they did during those troublesome times. They had shown the power of God and had preached, "Thus saith the Lord!"

These two will receive glorified bodies like Christ's. When they come alive, they will ascend into heaven as Christ did two thousand years ago. Those who are "raptured" before the seven-year Tribulation have glorified bodies; and these two also will ascend into the heavens. The media will cover this. It surely will be a miracle and wonder that only God could perform. God still does amazing things!

The Coming of the Earthquake

Revelation 11:13 says that there will be an earthquake so strong that it will bring down a tenth of the city. Seven thousand people will die. Yet, praise God, fear will come upon those who are still alive and escape the tragedy to "give glory to the God of heaven." It will be like the Twin Towers of 9/11 in 2001. People thought of the fallout of that terrorist attack. They imagined what it would have been like if they had been in those buildings, but because they lived through that tragedy, they glorified God that they were still alive.

In New York City, when 9/11 happened, both Jews and others were affected. That is what it will be like in the Tribulation time. In a time of a natural disaster, people often turn to Jesus as Savior because of the tragedy. While people may put off their decision for Christ at other times, tragedy makes them think about death. It is my prayer, and hopefully yours also, that many will be saved from sin. That seven-year Tribulation time will be scary, and it will be hard to claim Christ as Savior with so much deception and diplomatic unrest.

More Deceit of Satan, the Antichrist, and the False Prophet

In the next chapters of Revelation, persecution will increase for the country of Israel and Jews all over the world. There are different interpretations of some of these chapters, and I will not go into detail about all the events to follow. The primary purpose of the "evil one," Satan, the old dragon (Revelation 12:9) will be to thwart the peaceful existence of God's chosen people of Israel. The descendants of Abraham, Isaac, and Jacob are these chosen people who had received the everlasting covenant of God. Revelation 12 continues that God will cast out Satan from ever coming back to heaven to accuse the saints and report their evil deeds (as he did with Job in chapter 1 and chapter 2). God allows Satan to roam the earth, tempt people, and give words of evil terror to some. Satan also accuses Christians before heaven's throne.

We read that God will kick Satan out of His heaven, and this old serpent will be cast down to the earth, not to return to heaven ever again (12:10). Because of this situation, the persecution of the Jews will step up a notch. The scriptures say that Satan will know that his time will be shortened before he is cast in the abyss during the Millennium (Revelation 20:1–2). He wants to wreak havoc all over the world.

The escalation of evil and dominance of wickedness multiply the tension of Satan's work and the wrath of God on the sinful people of the earth. That is why they call the last half of the seven-year Tribulation the "Great Tribulation." As mentioned in earlier chapters, Satan will empower and possess an Antichrist who will take a seat of power. That world leader will bring chaos and delusion among the peoples of the world, and they will follow his advice and dictatorship.

This Antichrist will take dominance over the world and get nations to follow his every command. The religious, ecumenical world will befriend him. We read in prophecy that the "false prophet" and other dignitaries will promote and follow his every move. Because of his fame, he will set up an image of himself. He will speak forth a daily message with his plans and goals for the one world power and will give solutions to economic poverty, natural disaster, pandemics, thieves, scams, hacking, and trade. People will be devoted to the problem solver and dictator. They will even bow to and worship this earthly imposter (Revelation 13:4). He will set up a "chip" code (SIM card sort of chip under people's skin of their foreheads or hands). People will buy and sell without currency or credit cards. The scripture makes it clear that he will set up a "666 mark of the beast" for those in market trading around the world and even in local grocery stores and malls (Revelation 13:16–18).

The "dragon" (Satan), the serpent of evil, will initiate all the plans. He will use this puppet of a world leader to dominate and persecute God's protection over His chosen people (the Jews) and born-again Christians alike. He is the one mentioned earlier who will get many nations to come to the battle to annihilate the nation of Israel in the battle of Armageddon.

These persecutions, temptations, and trials will be very hard on the Jews and Christians with millions of beheadings, torture, and deaths during those troublesome seven years of tribulation.

> And unless those days were shortened, no flesh would be saved; but for the elect's sake, those days will be shortened. (Matthew 24:22)

Praise God that they will be relieved of the pain and sorrow of the Tribulation. There will be a time that the victorious King will be coming to bring down all principalities and powers of the beast, false prophet, and dreadful Satan. All three will have their final judgment and placement in the lower parts of the "lake of fire," which will burn with brimstone for eternity (Revelation 21:8). God banishes them, but His saints and chosen ones will live altogether with Him eternally in His "New Jerusalem" heaven.[17]

CHAPTER 7

CHRIST'S GLORY AS THE VICTORIOUS COMING KING

They shall speak of the glory of Your kingdom and talk
of Your power; to make known to the sons of men His
mighty acts, and the glorious majesty of His Kingdom.
—Psalm 145:11–12

Prophecies for the Kingdom Coming True

Revelation 14–18 presents some of the closing "wrath of God" that He will pour out on the whole world. Many people will still follow the "beast" (Antichrist) even though there is torment, disease, and pestilence. These are the ending months of God's cups of indignation upon those people who have taken the mark of the beast, the Antichrist.

The Nations Coming to Megiddo

This prophecy brings us to the gathering of the nations with the Antichrist. The nations will bring their weaponry to the Middle East and particularly to the Valley of Megiddo for the fierce overtake of the countryside of Israel:

> Then the sixth angel poured out his bowl (of wrath) on the great river Euphrates, and its water was dried up so that the way of the kings from the east might be prepared. (Revelation 16:12)

Signs of this great invitation and devilish words go out to prompt kings to bring their armies and missiles. Verse 14 says, "Which go out to the kings of the earth and of the whole world to gather them to the battle of that great day of God Almighty." Verse 16 sums it all up, to give us the correct name of the battle and the place: "And they gathered them together to the places called in Hebrew, 'Armageddon.'"

The Siege of Jerusalem

Zechariah 14 announces the siege of Jerusalem in the "Day of the Lord." Dr. John Walvoord and Dr. Roy Zuck have some good quotes here:

> The "Day of the LORD" is a theme occurring many times in the Old Testament. The "Day of the LORD" relates to the severe judgments in the Tribulation, as well as those accompanying the Second Advent. The spoil which will be divided is the valuables in Jerusalem and the surrounding area that will be taken and shared by the Gentile armies "in your midst."[18]

The invaders will feel secure (Zechariah 14:1–2).

The Nations Gathering

There is a gathering of Gentile confederation of troops from many nations that are induced from Satan, demonic forces, the world dictatorial Antichrist, and the false prophet (Revelation 16:13–14).

> Behold, I will make Jerusalem a cup of drunkenness to all the surrounding peoples, when they lay siege against Judah and Jerusalem. And it shall happen in that day that I will make Jerusalem a very heavy stone for all peoples; all who would heave it away will surely be cut in pieces, though all nations of the earth are gathered against it. (Zechariah 12:2–3)

The text in chapter 12 states that the people of Judah and Jerusalem will be emboldened with strength and power to resist the surge or siege of their region (vv. 6–8). God will still be in control even when nations gather. He knows the beginning of this pending siege and ending defeat. "For I will gather the nations to battle against Jerusalem" (Zechariah 14:2a). "It shall be in that day that I will seek to destroy all the nations that come against Jerusalem" (12:9). The Gentile troops will obtain an advantage of control of Judea and the capital, but the coming King Jesus will make a fast and potent end of their rampage of the region (14:2b).

The Messiah's Intervention

The pending and ever hopeful intervention of the coming Messiah and coming King Jesus will "go forth" or "go out" to battle. The Hebrew word is: *yatsa'* /yaw·tsaw/] v. A primitive root; the AV (KJV) translates as to go "out," "forth," "to proceed, to cause to go or come out, bring out, lead out" (Zechariah 14:3).[19]

The Lord Jesus Christ will go forth and out to battle. He will fight as a warrior in the Armageddon battle to lead the way with His holy ones, angels, and saints for a victory (Matthew 25:31; Zechariah 14:5c; Revelation 19:13–15). After such triumph over the Gentile enemies and weaponry, the coming King will still be riding on His white horse to the top of the Mount of Olives (14:4). He will descend as the prophecy states from His ascension event (Acts 1:11–12) to set foot on the mount just adjacent to the holy city of Jerusalem (v. 4).

Jesus's intervention will be as a conquering "Victor" over the military enemy. His righteous anger of wrath will come in a timely fashion for His beloved people, Israel, and the city of Jerusalem. The fallout of His fury is filled with blood (Revelation 19:11–18; Isaiah 34). The dread and doom will influence so many in the Middle East and the area surrounding Jerusalem.

> For the indignation of the LORD is against all nations, and the fury against all their armies; He has utterly destroyed them. He has given them over to the slaughter. (Isaiah 34:2)

Christ's accomplishment and intervention are the hallmarks of His "Second Coming" in "power and great glory" (Mark 13:26). Jesus coming will show the heartfelt love for His chosen people in Jerusalem:

> But the remnant of the people shall not be cut off from the city. (Zechariah 14:2c)

The aftermath of our Lord Jesus Christ touching His feet on the Mount of Olives will be an earthquake (Zechariah 14:4). Miraculously, the mount will split into two from east to west by direct intervention of the coming divine King. The earthquake will form a valley eastward from Jerusalem as far as the Jordan River, through which the remnant of Jews will flee. The Lord calls the valley "My mountain valley" (Zechariah14:5).

Scripture says the Judean people will flee in terror of their lives as they did in the days of King Uzziah. Seemingly, a tragedy of an earthquake happened in the reign of Uzziah. Yet, Amos the prophet did not mention any escape from harm during his time since he "saw (many events) concerning Israel during the days of Uzziah" (Amos 1:1). Amos and other writers of the historical books did not cite earthquakes throughout the days of King Uzziah's days as this prophetic event states in Zechariah 14.

The Establishment of the Messianic Kingdom

At the heart of Zechariah 14 is the affirmation that "the LORD shall be King over all the earth." He will be accepted as the "one LORD" (v. 9). This grand pronouncement is set in the context of changes in illumination, climate, and geography, which God will bring on Jerusalem, Palestine, and, no doubt, the whole earth during the Millennium.

The Passage of Zechariah 14:6–7

> The beginning day of the Millennium will be a
> special day, without day or night. The dark clouds
> attending the divine judgments will be replaced by
> illuminating light when the evening comes.

My thought is the evening "light" (v. 7) will be the divine radiance of the supper of the Lamb, the grand reception of the Groom (King Jesus) and His Bride. There will be divine wonders at Christ's Second Advent (Isaiah 3:10; 34:4; Joel 2:10, 30–31; 3:15; Matthew 24:29).

The Passage of Zechariah 14:8

> And in that day, it shall be that living waters shall
> flow from Jerusalem, half of them toward the

eastern sea, and half of them toward the western sea; in both summer and winter it shall occur.

If anyone studies the potential of water flow from the mountains of Turkey and Lebanon, they note that there are springs of underground water supply. Much of the Litani River and rainfall off Mount Hermon flows into the upper Jordan River and then into the Sea of Galilee. Yet in some way, King Hezekiah was able to make an aqueduct to flow fresh spring water into the citadel of Jerusalem (2 Kings 18:17). Various tributaries of water flow and irrigation supplies have faced the desert regions of the Middle East. Yet for Israel, God has an underground supply like spring water under the Mount of Olives from this earthquake (Zechariah 14:5). On this victorious day of the coming King Jesus, water will flow east to the Dead Sea and west to the Mediterranean Sea. There will be an abundance of future irrigation sources to fertilize the land of Israel (Isaiah 35:1–3; Amos 9:13–14). We will touch upon this flowing spring of healing river (Ezekiel 47:9) in a further chapter discussing the agricultural abundance during these thousand years of prosperity and rule of the "King of kings and Lord of lords" (Revelation 19:16).

The War of Armageddon

Armageddon [Arm-ah-GED-un] is also known as the Mountain of Megiddo. Mount Megiddo's site has witnessed many of Israel's battles: (1) the fate of world governments (Psalm 2:7–9), (2) a coming decisive battle (Daniel 11:36–45), and (3) historic wars (Judges 5:19).

Mount Megiddo will be the site of the final battle of this age in which God intervenes to destroy the armies of Satan and to cast Satan into the bottomless pit (Revelation 16:16; 20:1). Scholars disagree about the exact location of this place, but the most likely possibility is the valley between Mount Carmel and the city of Jezreel to the east.

This reference index of "Nelson's Quick Reference Topical Bible Index" helps give their viewpoint of where the battle of Armageddon will take place:

> This valley (known as the Valley of Jezreel and sometimes referred to as the Plain of Esdraelon) was the crossroads of two ancient trade routes and thus was a strategic military site and scene of many ancient battles. The "valley-plain of Megiddo" (2 Chronicles 35:22) has witnessed decisive battles, from one fought by Pharaoh Tuthmosis III in 1468 BC to that of Lord Allenby of Megiddo in 1917. Napoleon called it "the cockpit of the world"; ("the ideal battlefield"). The "mountains of Israel" will witness Gog's defeat in Ezekiel 39:1–4. This region may be in the apostle John's and many other commentator's minds when the nations come to battle.[20]

In history, the "tell" (the layers of civilizations built on a hill) of Megiddo and the surrounding valley became a symbol of the apocalypse between God and the forces of evil. According to Revelation 16, the last "bowl" judgments are included in the battle of Armageddon, "the cup of the wine of the fierceness of His [God's] wrath" (v. 19). God will pour out His wrath on the forces of evil to be defeated.

The Meaning of Armageddon

The word "Armageddon" in Hebrew comes with a combination from the Greek "*Harmagedōn*," which has the Hebrew words for "mount" (=har) "the place of Armageddon" (Revelation 16:16). Latin is *Hermagedon*; Greek is *Magedon*). This word comes from the root word of the location of the city "Mount Megiddo" and the valley nearby. Some may say the word is just a symbolic word for war and mischief. Yet, all in all, the battle will come with the influence and domineering of Satan and His forces.[21]

In Revelation 16:13–14, John sees three frog-like spirits issuing from the mouth of the dragon, the beast, and the false prophet, which are referred to as Satan's counterfeit trinity. These demonic spirits perform miracles to deceive the world's rulers and lure them to a climactic battle on the great day of God Almighty (16:14–16). The Lord interjects a special blessing on the Tribulation saints, who are watching for His Return. They have kept themselves pure from the idolatrous worship of that day (v. 15). Christ will come to the Tribulation of unbelievers as a thief, unexpectedly and causing loss and destruction. The apostle Paul speaks of this in 1 Thessalonians 5:1–2: "For you know quite well that the day of the Lord will come unexpectedly, like a thief in the night."

The Demonic Forces at Armageddon

While the meaning of this symbolic presentation is clear, there is a significant problem involved in what the demons do. Satan will establish the coming world government in the Great Tribulation (Revelation 13:2). The counterfeit trinity unites to provoke the nations of the world to gather for this war of "Armageddon." Yet, the war is a form of rebellion against the world ruler. Why would satanic forces be let loose to destroy the newly created world emperor (Antichrist)? [22]

The answer seems to be in the events that follow. Satan, knowing that the Second Coming of Christ is near, will gather all the military might of the world into the Holy Land to resist the arrival of the Son of Man, Jesus, who will return to the Mount of Olives (Zechariah 14:4). Though the nations may be deceived into entering the war in the hope of gaining world political power, the satanic purpose is to combat the armies from heaven (introduced in Revelation 19) at the Second Coming of Christ.

The war is said to continue right up to the day of the Second Coming and involves house-to-house combat in Jerusalem itself on the day of the Lord's return (Zechariah 14:1–3). The reference to "the battle" (Greek *ton polemon*, Revelation 16:14) is probably better translated "the war." Thus, it is better to speak of "the war of Armageddon" (v. 16) rather than "the battle of Armageddon." The war will be going on for some time, but the climax will come at Christ's Second Advent. [23]

Accordingly, John heard the warning coming from Christ Himself:

> Behold, I am coming like a thief. Blessed is he who watches and keeps his garments, lest he walk naked and they see his shame. (Revelation 16:15)

Christ's return is like the coming of a thief. It implies suddenness and unpreparedness as far as unbelievers are concerned. Just as Christians are not to be surprised by the Rapture of the Church (1 Thessalonians 5:4), so we should be anticipating His return. Blessing is promised to the godly ones who are prepared for the coming of the Lord. Are you ready for Christ's return? Do you have the righteous clothing that God Himself supplies? Are you prepared for the entrance into the Millennium?

The Bowl Judgments to Come

The ending verses of Revelation 16:16–21 are to be taken as a whole. The sixth and seventh bowls of the wrath of God are preparations for the final act of judgment before the Second Coming. It is the later stage of development related to the River Euphrates being dried up and all the earthquakes and disasters that fall upon the earth and humanity (vv. 12–21). The time factor between the sixth trumpet and the sixth bowl is comparatively short.[24]

When the seventh angel completes his bowl judgment, a loud voice from the throne of heaven will pronounce, "It is done" (Revelation 16:17). It could very well be the same as "Babylon the great is fallen" (Revelation 18:2). It will indicate the wrath of God is complete as far as the Tribulation period is concerned. The earth will be utterly ruined with lightning, thunder, earthquakes, plagues, hailstones, and cities shaken (vv. 17–21).

Christ Will Return in Glory

John first describes Jesus as the Conqueror (Revelation 19:11–16), and then he describes His conquests (Revelation 19:17–20:3). The rider on the white horse is the actual Savior and Lord, Jesus Christ. He is not coming this time "in the air" to take His people home (1 Thessalonians 4:13–18) but to "the earth" with His people, to conquer His enemies and establish His Kingdom. The return of Christ will be magnificent. He will be a mighty Warrior, the conquering King, coming to earth with all power and glory.

The Names of the Conquering King

Note the emphasis on Jesus's names in Revelation 19:11–13, 16. He is "Faithful and True" (Revelation 3:14), in contrast to "the beast" who was unfaithful (he broke the covenant with Israel) and false (he ruled employing deception and idolatry). Suffering saints need to be reminded that God is faithful and will not desert them because His promises are true.

Perhaps the secret name of Jesus in Revelation 19:12 is the same as the "new name" mentioned in Revelation 3:12. The name will be given when the New Jerusalem will be coming down out of heaven

(Revelation 21:2). For now, we do not know what this name is. It may be a surprise to all of us, but it is exciting to know that even in the new heaven, we shall learn new things about our Lord Jesus. What we do know is that "new name" will be glorious, bringing amazement to our hearts and souls.

Revelation 19:13 says, "His name is called the Word of God." The "Word of God" is one of the familiar names of our Lord in scripture (John 1:1–14). Just as we reveal our minds and hearts to others with words, so the Father reveals Himself to us through His Son, the incarnate Word (the Word in the flesh). Just as letters make up words, Jesus Christ, the "Word" is the first and the last letter of the alphabet. He is the "Alpha and Omega" (Revelation 21:6; 22:13). "Alpha and Omega" are the first and last letters of the Greek alphabet. He is the beginning and end of the divine alphabet of God's revelation to us (Revelation 1:8, 11).

The Word of God is "living and powerful" (Hebrews 4:12). What is more, it fulfills His purposes on earth (Revelation 17:17; also note Revelation 6:11; 10:7; 15:1). Jehovah Himself says, "I am watching to see that My Word is fulfilled" (Jeremiah 1:12 NIV84). Just as the Word was the Father's agent in Creation (John 1:1–3), so the Word is His agent for judgment and consummation.

Christ's most important name is "King of kings, and Lord of lords" (Revelation 19:16), which is His victorious name (Revelation 17:14). The name recalls references such as Daniel 2:47 and Deuteronomy 10:17. Paul used this same title for our Lord Jesus Christ in 1 Timothy 6:15. This title speaks of Christ's sovereignty since all kings and lords must submit to Him. No matter who was on the throne of the Roman Empire, on that day—and for all future days—Jesus Christ is Lord and King!

The Conquest of the King

As John gazed into heaven, he saw Christ on a white horse (Revelation 19:11). The white horse is a sign of His coming triumph. It was customary for a triumphant Roman general to parade on the "Via Sacra," a main thoroughfare of Rome, followed by evidence of his victory in the form of spoils of war and captives (2 Corinthians 2:14). The white horse is a symbol of Christ's victory over the forces of wickedness in the world.

"Faithful and True" is the name of the horse's rider. John declared, "With justice, He judges and makes war" (v. 11 NIV84). His piercing judgment of sin is indicated in the words "His eyes are like blazing fire" (Revelation 1:14). The "many crowns" evidence His right to rule (19:12). "King of kings, and Lord of lords" is written on His robe at His thigh (1 Timothy 6:15; Revelation 17:14; 19:16). The rider is Jesus Christ, returning to the earth in glory. He is coming as Judge, which is further supported by the fact that He wears a robe dipped in blood. He has been given authority and is worthy to judge the world (Revelation 19:13; 14:20; Isaiah 63:2–3).

The Coming of the King and His Armies of Heaven

The many crowns (diadems) on Jesus's head indicate His magnificent rule and sovereignty. As I said previously, the vesture dipped in blood speaks of judgment and probably relates to Isaiah 63:1–6 and Revelation 14:20, the conquest of His enemies. It is not our Lord's blood that marks His vesture; it is that of His foes.

The sharp sword is a symbol of God's Word (Revelation 19:21; see also Ephesians 6:17; Hebrews 4:12; Revelation 1:16). Christ will consume the enemy "with the spirit of His mouth" (2 Thessalonians

2:8; Isaiah 11:4). Earlier, "the rod of iron" was mentioned (Revelation 2:27; 12:5) as a symbol of His justice. The image of the winepress must be associated with the judgment at Armageddon (Revelation 14:14–20; Isaiah 63:1–6).

Jesus is not alone in His conquest since the armies of heaven ride with Him. Who are they? The angels are a part of this army (Matthew 25:31), but so also are the saints (1 Thessalonians 3:13; 2 Thessalonians 1:7, 10). Jude describes the same scene (Jude 1:14–15). The word "saints" means "holy ones" in Jude 14 and could refer to believers or angels or both. It will be unnecessary for His army to fight since Christ Himself will defeat the enemy through these victories.

The Destruction of the Wicked

The enemy warriors have assembled to fight "against the LORD and against his Anointed One" (Psalm 2:1–3 NIV84). However, their weapons prove futile. The battle turns out to be a slaughter, a supper for the scavenger birds. The first half of Revelation 19 describes the "Marriage Supper of the Lamb." The last half describes the "Great Supper of God" with the enemies of King Jesus who died in Armageddon as meat for the birds (Matthew 24:28; Luke 17:37; Revelation 19:17–18). Warlords will be lured to the battle site by demons sent by Satan to assemble the armies of the world to fight the armies of heaven (Revelation 16:12–16).

In addition to using the sword for striking down, Jesus will use an iron scepter for ruling (Psalm 2:9; Revelation 2:27). Christ is described as the One who "treads the winepress of the fury of the fierceness and wrath of Almighty God" (Revelation 19:15b; see also Revelation 14:19–20). This scene is a dramatic indication of the awfulness of the impending judgment. Matthew 24:30 indicates that those on earth will be witnesses of this impressive scene. Here again, the media will cover it quickly before that final judgment day.

The word "flesh" occurs six times in Revelation 19:17–21. John's immediate reference is to the human body being eaten by carnivore birds (v. 17). A definite meaning of "flesh" here is that humankind is frail in the flesh without strength or might. The Bible has nothing good to say about fallen human beings. God's words before the Flood were: "My spirit shall not always strive with man, for that he also is flesh" (Genesis 6:3; John 3:6; 6:63; Romans 7:18; Philippians 3:3). "All flesh is as grass" (1 Peter 1:24) and must be judged. Hebrews 9:27 does well here: "And as it is appointed for men to die once, but after this the judgment." The "flesh" of men's bodies will die and be judged someday by God. Adam's sin (Genesis 3), until now for all mankind has God's pending judgment at one's death and a second death of judgment into the "lake of fire" (Revelation 20:11:15).

The Defeat of the Armies and Kings of the Earth

The armies of the earth are no match for the troops from heaven, especially Jesus Christ. The sharp sword in Christ's mouth (Revelation 19:15) is symbolic of His authoritative word of command that destroys the earth's armies by divine power. Seemingly millions of men, their horses, and weaponry will be killed instantly (Revelation 19:18). In keeping with this, John recorded that he saw "an angel standing in the sun, who cried in a loud voice, saying to all birds that fly in the midst of heaven, 'Come and gather together for the supper of the great God,' that you may eat the flesh … of mighty men, the flesh of horses and those who sit on them, and the flesh of all people free and slave, both small and great" (Revelation 19:17–18). They were slain by Christ Jesus, the King.

All that our Lord must do is speak the Word, and "the sword of His mouth" will devour His enemies. He will defeat the "beast" (the Antichrist) and the false prophet (Revelation 19:20). Since Satan's "henchmen" are the leaders of the revolt, it is only right that they are captured and confined. The beast and the false prophet are the first persons to be cast into the lake of fire as their final judgment (Revelation 19:20). Satan will follow a thousand years later (Revelation 20:10), to be joined by those whose names are not found in the Book of Life (20:15). The lake of fire is the final and permanent place of punishment for all who refuse to submit to the Lord Jesus Christ (v.15).

CHAPTER 8

FIRST THINGS FIRST
FOR GOD'S GLORY

Then comes the end, when He delivers the
kingdom to God the Father, when He puts an
end to all rule and all authority and power.
—1 Corinthians 15:24

I n this chapter, we want to look at the various judgments
that King Jesus will perform. He will deal with the world of
unrighteousness that opposes God's righteousness and anger as
He pours out His wrath during the seven-year Tribulation.

Some of the earlier destruction that comes on the earth is
God's anger displayed on the economic and political rule of many
ungodly countries. One of these places is called the "harlot," which
represents the future city of Babylon (Revelation 17:5). God will
dole out judgment against the Antichrist and the false prophet's
great powers to manipulate and control matters during the Great
Tribulation. This Great Babylon of influence will move the stock
markets and commerce gains to great heights. Their impact and
control, however, will come to a halt by the destruction of the angels
that God will send to bring the last of the bowl judgments on planet
earth (Revelation 16–18).

Dr. Joseph M. Stowell, in *Kingdom Conflict*, explains what

happens in history when mankind builds a city for themselves, like the Tower of Babel in Genesis 11. First, they gathered to build a structure to reach the heavens. Secondly, they gathered the one common language of people in a city to make a "name for themselves." Thirdly, they became independent from God and glorified themselves."[25]

The descendants of Noah intended to gather, rather than to scatter, over the earth as God had commanded (Genesis 9:1). Dr. Stowell also continued to say for any city in our day and age:

> A city is a monument to the man and his glory ...skyscrapers stand as monuments to our (mankind's) genius. "They are our glory." The city is the marketplace of materialism and offers us waters from the wells of pride, self-sufficiency, and sensuous living ... The city (living) makes it easier to lose an awareness of God, while becoming more independent from Him, more self-sufficient, and more proud of their accomplishments.[26]

Modern "Babylon" will be built with the combined efforts of Satan's strategies and men's commerce and self-gratification. Men want to make a name for themselves. Satan will attack the lordship of Christ and insult Christians and Jews alike. Satan will bring citywide pride to the highest degree (Revelation 18:6–9). The distraction of city life with its appeal impedes the work of God. Satan loves to sabotage God's children with the pleasures of life.

God's Judgment on the Fall of the Great City of Babylon

The great city of Babylon is just one of the many judgments from God in bringing King Jesus closer to His triumphal day. He will have His final day of destruction against all the military forces of the world (Revelation 19). The world's leaders will be against God and His people, Israel, in the Holy Land. God will especially pour out His wrath during the last half of the seven-year Tribulation. He has His messenger angel to declare the judgment on the center of evil in the social and prestigious influences in the whole world.

The Proclamation of the Angel

This next section is Dr. Walvoord and Dr. Zuck's view and interpretation of this great revelation of the destruction of Babylon by an angel coming down from heaven (Revelation 18:1–2 NIV84).

> The angel's message is summarized: 'Fallen! Fallen is Babylon the Great!' The question has been raised as to whether or not this is another view of the same destruction mentioned in 17:16–17. A comparison of chapters 17 and 18 reveals that these are different events. The woman in chapter 17 was associated with the political power but was not the political power itself, and her destruction apparently brought no mourning from the earth. By contrast the destruction of Babylon in chapter 18 brings loud lamentation from the earth's political and economic powers. Instead of being destroyed and consumed by the ten kings, here the destruction seems to come from an earthquake, and it is probable that this is an enlarged explanation of what was described in 16:19–21.[27]

In Revelation 18, the angel will instruct the people of God to leave this "Babylon the Great." They will escape the judgment to come to the city (vv. 2–4). The city will receive torture and grief combined with her glory and luxury, in which she boasted that she was a queen (vv. 5–7). Death, mourning, famine, and fire will come to the city in one day (v. 8). The contrast of the two chapters and statements about the two characteristics of this future city of "Babylon" shows its destruction in different aspects and degrees. Chapters 17 and 18 show different aspects of the judgment.

The Pronouncement of Being "Fallen"

The phrase "is fallen, is fallen" adds a dramatic effect to the announcement, and it suggests a dual judgment: upon ecclesiastical Babylon, "the harlot" in Revelation 17, and political Babylon in Revelation 18. This thought is amplified in verse 6 when God announces that Babylon will receive "double" for her many sins.

Dr. Warren Wiersbe's *Bible Exposition Commentary* gives some cross-references we find for Revelation 18:

> The Church, the Bride of the Lamb, is the habitation of God (Ephesians 2:22). Babylon, on the other hand, is the habitation of Satan (Revelation 18:2). This parallels the judgment on ancient Babylon (Isaiah 13:21ff; Jeremiah 51:37ff). Furthermore, the apostle John called the city "a cage of every unclean and hateful bird" (Revelation 18:2). In Christ's parable of the Sower, He also used the birds as a picture of Satan (Matthew 13:31–32).[28]

These sorts of unclean scavenger birds, as we know them, are vultures, eagles, ravens, and blackbirds. They are the kind of birds that are usually on the sides of the highways eating roadkill flesh. In the future, the blood of evangelical prophets will be thrown into their cages for dead meat (18:2). If King Darius of the Persian Empire had his "lion's den," this Babylon city will have its vulture cages (Daniel 6:16). Revelation 18:20 says that the sent ones of the Tribulation time (missionaries) will rejoice that the great city of Babylon will be destroyed. The same vultures that are multiplied in the Tribulation will be called to the "the supper of the great God" (Revelation 19:17). They will eat the carcasses of all the mighty enemy soldiers lying all over the ground after Christ's victorious win over Armageddon (v. 18).

This judgment will come because of the Babylonian worldwide political-economic system. It will pollute the whole world. As in the judgment of "the harlot" (Revelation 17), the sin is that of "fornication" against God Himself. The system of Babylon has and will intoxicate the people of the world with all the riches and pleasures it will offer. It will cater to those who are "lovers of pleasures rather than lovers of God" (2 Timothy 3:4).

If you read Revelation 18 carefully, you see that the great city of Babylon will be burned by a possible meteorite that the sent angel will use to execute God's wrath upon their sin (Revelation 18:21). It says that the boulder will be thrown into the sea, and the splash, with the possible heat of the molten rock from not being burned up in the atmosphere, sets the city on fire. God judges that evil commercial city. Could it be a port city of the ships that will be staying their distance in the ocean? Those on the ships will watch the city burn and lament over the luxurious cargo as well as the bars where they spent happy hours at the port (Revelation 18:11–18). God's judgments are sure, and evil will be dealt with a vengeance in those last days of the wrath of God before the Millennial Kingdom is established (Revelation 18:20).[29]

All these despicable evil doings on the earth during the Tribulation will need the final judgments of God, so Christ can rule in His Kingdom fully. Satan knows his day of judgment is near (Revelation 12:12), and he uses all the deceit and ungodliness he can muster. John the apostle said that this "dragon, that serpent of old" (Revelation 20:2), is the same evil one mentioned by the apostle Paul as the "prince of the power of the air" (Ephesians 2:2) on earth. He deceives the world into his luxury and glamour of corruption and abominations against God.

There is an order we find here in the book of Revelation before Jesus comes to display His glory with His angels and saints. He is all business with His judgment at the end of the Tribulation. He will get rid of judges and all evil leaders who have corrupted the earth with their influence, having been seduced by Satan.[30]

Christ Judging the Sheep and Goats

Now when Jesus was anticipating going to the cross to give His life a ransom for people's sin, He told His twelve disciples some of His future judgments. This scripture is a part of His sermon on the Mount of Olives, near the end of His life:

> When the Son of Man comes in His glory, and all the[j] holy angels with Him, then He will sit on the throne of His glory. All the nations will be gathered before Him, and He will separate them one from another, as a shepherd divides his sheep from the goats. (Matthew 25:31–32)

This separation is like a shepherd dividing the two species in the evening when they come in from grazing. According to the Jewish apocalyptic literature, there is a future judgment. As the verses just stated, a shepherd from time to time would make a distinction in segregating the two animal groups from the pasture lands.

Dr. Craig Keener describes this separation and its apocalyptic implications in this manner:

> Since the natural grazing patterns during a given day, would mingle both sheep and goats together in seeking the best areas of pasture. Yet later, the Palestinian shepherds would normally have to separate the sheep from the goats at night, because goats need to be warm at night while sheep prefer the open air. Sheep were more valuable than goats,

and the characteristics like this may have influenced how these terms and interpretation would be understood here in God's Holy Scriptures. (Ezekiel 34:17)[31]

The End-Time Judgment of the Nations

Joel 3:1–21 gives a sketch of the future judgment day as described as a Valley of Jehoshaphat, or the "valley of decision" (Joel 3:14), to come:

> For behold, in those days and at that time, when I bring back the captives of Judah and Jerusalem. I will also gather all nations, and bring them down to the Valley of Jehoshaphat; and I will enter into judgment with them on account of My people, My heritage Israel, whom they have scattered the nations; they have also divided up My land. (Joel 3:1–2)

In Dr. David Jeremiah's Study Bible's footnotes, the judgment day is pending. Joel 3 is a carryover from Joel 2:32: "That whoever calls on the name of the LORD shall be saved." God is looking for a repentant heart for those who follow in His righteous ways. He will also restore all things to Judah and Jerusalem. Joel 3:1 states that "in those days, and at that time," God will gather and bring the nations down to the Valley of Jehoshaphat (Joel 2:2a, 12). Then He calls it the "valley of decision" (3:14).

> The "valley of decision" is another name for the Valley of Jehoshaphat, where God will judge the nations for scattering His covenant people and for dividing up His land. It is better understood as "the

valley of the verdict" since it will be too late for any
of those people to make a decision: judgment has
come.[32]

"The Hebrew word for Jehoshaphat is "je hŏsh' a făt" (יְהוֹשָׁפָט
עֵמֶק; LXX κοιλαδα Ιωσαφατ, means: 'God shall judge, or Jehovah
has judged."[33] Dr. Jeremiah believes that this meaning of the Hebrew
word (*yehoshafat*), "God has judged," is judging, and will judge the
nations of the world. "The Lord judges." The Major and Minor
Prophets mention "in that day or days" (future time), there will be
a "valley of decision" coming on all the ethnic peoples of the earth
(Joel 3:2, 12, 14). Christ's statement in Matthew 25:31–32 confirms
that "all nations will be gathered before Him (the Son of Man,
Jesus)." Joel 3:2 also indicates this.

We can conclude from the context and the final fulfillment of
Christ's teaching about a future joining of nations that there will be a
division between the righteous and unrighteous people on a specific
day. Dr. Albert Barnes also denotes that:

> This "valley of decision" is a "sharp, severe
> judgment." This valley is the same as mentioned
> previously as "the Valley of Jehoshaphat." Yet for
> this further name denotes the strictness of God's
> judgment (v.14). The word signifies "cut," then
> "decided."[34]

It will be the conquering Jesus who will severely punish and
divide people into their respected destinies. There is a division of
those saved individuals as God's sheep and the punishment of the
evil "goats" going to their everlasting punishment (Matthew 25:46).[35]

Joel chapter 3 has so many indicators of judgment and reigning
by Jesus Christ as the coming King. God will call the unbelievers
to the "valley of decision" of God's judgment. God will gather the
unbelievers to give an account for scattering the Hebrew people

(selling as slaves, vv. 3, 6–7) among the nations and dividing up God's Promised Land (v. 2d). The Jews are God's special people whom the nations have treated with contempt and inhumanity. God will arouse the unbelievers to come, and He will judge them in the Valley of Jehoshaphat (v. 2a). It will be in that place that Jesus the King will divide and mandate the destiny of all the nations (vv. 11–12). He will be the righteous Jew's refuge of safety, and they will dwell on His holy mountain, Zion (vv. 17, 21).

The harvest of souls also has the comparison of bringing in the sheaves of wheat and throwing the clusters of tares into the fire (Matthew 13:30). God decides to divide and make the verdict of the destination. This is the "valley of decision."

> For their wickedness is great. Multitudes, multitudes
> in the valley of decision! (Joel 3:13–14)

> And these will go away into everlasting punishment,
> but the righteous into eternal life. (Matthew 25:46)

This passage is so distinct regarding the coming judgment day before the millennial reign of the coming King.[36]

> I will gather all nations and bring them down to the
> Valley of Jehoshaphat. (Joel 3:2)

> It may be that the imagery is furnished by that
> great deliverance that God gave to Jehoshaphat,
> when "Ammon and Moab and Edom come against"
> him "to cast" them out (2 Chronicles 20:10–12);
> Jehoshaphat appealed to God, "O our God, wilt
> Thou not judge them?" and God said, "The battle
> is not yours, but God's" (v. 15) and God turned
> their swords, everyone, against the other, and none
> escaped.[37]

The millennial characteristics are all here in this Joel chapter three: 1} sun, moon, and stars darkened (v. 15), 2} the earth shaking under the thunderclaps of God's judgment (v. 16), 3} no foreigners will invade the land ever again (v. 17), 4} new wine and buttermilk will drip from Judah's hills (v. 18), 5} Egypt will be judged (v. 19), and 6} Judah and Jerusalem will be inhabited forever throughout all generations (v. 20). The ending of this great prophetic chapter is that "the LORD dwells in Zion" (Joel 3:21) forever! That climax is the desire of God's heart to dwell with His saints forever and ever in eternity (Revelation 21:3)!

Joel chapter three is about the end-times before the millennial reign of Jesus Christ. The nations will assemble in the vast plains near Megiddo for the battle of Armageddon and will prepare for war. Joel 3 talks about the assertion of the countries as they plot against Jerusalem and the surrounding region (Zechariah 14:2). The Israelites will surely fight, but when the enemies seem overwhelming and looting prevails, Christ, who is called "Faithful and True," will conquer with sharp words from His mouth (Revelation 19:13, 15).

> Proclaim this among the nations; Prepare for war! Wake up the mighty men, let all the men of war draw near, let them come up. Beat your plowshares into swords, and your pruning hooks into spears; let the weak say, "I am strong." Assemble and come, all you nations, and gather together all around. Cause Your mighty ones (warriors) to go down there, O LORD. Let the nations be wakened and come up to the Valley of Jehoshaphat; for there, I will sit to judge all the surrounding nations. Put in the sickle, for the harvest is ripe. Come, go down; for the winepress is full. The vats overflow—For their wickedness is great. Multitudes, multitudes in the valley of decision! For the day of the LORD is near in the valley of decision. (Joel 3:9–14)

Christ the King's judgment in the valley will be after the defeat of the Antichrist and his armies. It will draw near soon, very soon before the Marriage Supper of the Lamb and coronation:

> So, you shall know that I am the LORD your God, dwelling in Zion, My holy mountain ... For the LORD dwells in Zion. (Joel 3:17, 21)

The Placement of the Sheep

Looking back at the Olivet discourse, Matthew 25:33 states, "And He will set the sheep on His right hand, but the goats on the left." Ancient Jewish shepherds separated the sheep from the goats every evening, leading the sheep to the right and the goats to the left. The separation was part of their Jewish culture.

The heavenly Father gives the place of authority to Jesus on His right hand (Acts 7:55; Hebrews 8:3).

> Come, you blessed of My Father, inherit the kingdom prepared for you from the foundation of the world. (Matthew 25:34)

It is Jesus's judgment day for the nations. All the countries of the world will be represented for this judgment day. Jesus knows those who are His sheep. His sheep have their sins forgiven and are ready to enter the glorious Millennial Kingdom.

This dynamic parallel of Joel 3 and Matthew 25 sets the stage of happenings and sequence to the beginning of the rule and reign of Christ Jesus as King:

> My sheep hear My voice, and I know them, and they follow Me. And I give them eternal life, and

they shall never perish, neither shall anyone snatch them out of My hand. (John 10:27–28)

Oh, what a marvelous truth that both Jew and Gentile believers are secure in the hands of our Lord Jesus, the coming King.

The Placement of the Goats

So now, what about those "goats" (the unbelievers)? Where will they end up?

> Then He will also say to those on the left hand, "Depart from Me, you cursed, into everlasting fire prepared for the devil and his angels." (Matthew 25:41)

The Lord Jesus judges the unbelieving goats based on how they know Him and how they treated others. Dr. Craig Keener also said in *The IVP Bible Background Commentary:*

> In some Jewish apocalyptic texts, the nations would be judged for how they treated Israel. In the Bible, God also judged people for how they treated the poor. But given the use of "brothers" or "sisters" (Matthew 12:50; 28:10 "My brethren," the Greek term can include both genders) and perhaps "least" {being the poor} Matthew 5:19; 11:11; 18:4; 20:26; 23:11 or "least as a servant". This passage probably refers to receiving messengers of Christ. Such missionaries needed shelter, food, and help in imprisonment and other complications caused by persecution. Receiving them was like receiving Christ (Matthew 10:40–42). The judgment of all

nations thus had to be preceded by the kingdom coming among them (24:14).[38]

Those Taken and Those Left Behind

We know there is a coming snatching away of some, and others who will be left behind. Matthew 24–25 speaks so much of Christ's coming with signs, wonders, and mighty judgments. Believers and unbelievers alike have their specific destinations.

> Christ Jesus said, "Two men will be in the field: one will be taken and the other left. Two women will be grinding at the mill: one will be taken, and the other left. Watch, therefore, for you do not know what hour your Lord is coming." (Matthew 24:40–42)

This passage refers to the separation of the "sheep" (the believers) from the "goats" (the unbelievers). The one taken is the unbeliever who is not ready to go into the kingdom of the Millennium. The other one remains left behind on the earth to go into the presence of Christ's inauguration as King in Jerusalem. Remember, it is the context of Jesus's teaching here at the Mount of Olives, to give the revelation of His return to the earth (after the Tribulation), as opposed to the Rapture in the clouds before the Tribulation (1 Thessalonians 4:13–18). People and preachers alike have gotten this passage confused in the past.

The King Judges the Nations

This next section gives us an additional view of the above commentary elements. Dr. William MacDonald and Dr. Arthur

Farstad describe this judgment of the nations, in which there should be distinguishing components between the typical questions about the various "judgments" of God. These "judgments" are pending in the realm of a whole nation and individuals in various nations. Here are the renditions given of three judgments to come:

> 1. The Judgment Seat of Christ is a time of review and reward for believers only (Romans 14:10). It takes place after the Rapture in God's heaven for rewards to those who use their talents and spiritual gifts for the Lord (2 Corinthians 5:9–10).

> This judgment is also called the "Bema Seat of Christ." ("The Ancient Greek *bēma* (βῆμα) means both 'platform' and 'step,' being derived from '*bainein*" (βαίνειν), 'to go'). The original use of the "bema" in Athens was as a tribunal from which orators addressed the citizens as well as the courts of law. The bema is a tribunal for rewards. In the large Olympic arenas, there was an elevated *seat* (emphasis mine), on which the judge of the contest sat. After the contests were over, rewards and honor were given in gold, silver, and bronze medals.[39]

> This Bema judgment will be tested by "fire" to come from the crucible metal pot to come forth as gold or silver (1 Corinthians 3:11–15). It will be like what the Old Testament patriarch, Job said, "But He (God) knows the way that I take; When He has tested me, I shall come forth as gold" (Job 23:10). Every Christian should have the same hope and desire to be well-pleasing in God's sight to be tested and come through the endurance principle "like gold" (James 5:11). This "judgment seat of Christ" should not

be confused with any of the "last day" judgments Jesus will have before the actual ushering into the Millennial Kingdom. Only true Christians have this reality check to be awarded for their service to their Savior, the Lord Jesus Christ (Hebrews 11:6).

2. The Judgment of the Nations, or Gentiles, Dr. Warren Wiersbe states in the *Believer's Bible Commentary* (the Greek words "nations" or "Gentiles" are usually interchangeable).

(This judgment) takes place on earth after Christ comes to reign, as Matthew 25:31 clearly states: "When the Son of Man comes in His glory, and all the holy angels with Him." If we are right in identifying it with Joel 3, the location is the Valley of Jehoshaphat, outside Jerusalem (3:2). The nations will be judged according to their treatment of Christ's Jewish brethren during the Tribulation (Joel 3:1, 2, 12–14; Matthew 25:31–46).[40]

3. The Judgment of the "Great White Throne" takes place directly after the thousand-year kingdom reign of Christ Jesus, the King. The wicked dead will be judged and cast ("consigned," MacDonald's word) to the "lake of fire" (Revelation 20:11–15). This is the final overall judgment given to all unbelievers whose names are not written in the "Book of Life" (Revelation 20:12, 15). Those judged are issued into everlasting punishment in the "lake of fire" (Matthew 25:46; Revelation 20:14).[41]

The Conclusions of Matthew 25:44–46

Dr. MacDonald and Dr. Farstad conclude answers to typical questions with excellent commentary:

> Thus, the goats go away into everlasting punishment, but the sheep into eternal life. But this raises two problems. First, the passage seems to teach those nations are saved or lost en masse. Second, the narrative creates the impression that the sheep are saved by good works, and the goats are condemned through failure to do good.
>
> As to the first difficulty, it must be remembered that God does deal with nations as such. Old Testament history abounds with instances of nations punished because of their sin (Isaiah 10:12–19; 47:5–15; Ezekiel 25:6–7; Amos 1:3, 6, 9, 11, 13; 2:1, 4, 6; Obadiah 10; Zechariah 14:1–5). It is not unreasonable to believe those nations will continue to experience divine retribution due to their sin. This does not mean that every single individual in the nation will be involved in the outcome, but that the principles of divine justice will be applied on a national, as well as an individual basis.[42]

These commentators added the full meaning to this ending of the Tribulation wrath of God upon humanity's evil. Jesus, the coming King, will judge truthfully and sharply those wicked and unbelieving scoundrels. The righteous and saved ones at the end of the seven-year Tribulation who endure in faithfulness will enter the Millennial Kingdom. Praise be to the "King of kings and Lord of lords" (Revelation 19:16).

CHAPTER 9

GLORY TO THE KING ON THE THRONE

But to the Son, He says: "Your throne, O God, is forever and
ever; A scepter of righteousness is the scepter of Your kingdom."
—Hebrews 1:8

C hrist taught on the Mount of Olives that all born-again
believers and followers of His were to be "watchful" for
His coming (Matthew 25:13). Jesus taught this truth in
the parable of the ten virgins. He concluded that five were wise
virgin friends of the bridegroom who were waiting and watching
for the coming of the groom. The other five were foolish ladies who
were not prepared for the marriage to take place at the groom's
house (Matthew 25:1–13). Jesus's sermon taught that all were to be
wise in waiting and expectantly watching for the timing of Christ's
Second Advent and His coming to sit on His majestic, judicial
throne rightfully.

Signs of Jesus's Appearing

Matthew 24 states the signs and happenings before Christ
Jesus's return. The visible cosmological incidents (earthquakes, earth

warming, meteorites, red moons, tsunamis, volcano eruptions, and pandemics) will tell us that the Son of Man, Jesus (the Groom and Judge) is coming soon:

> Then the sign of the Son of Man will appear in heaven, and then all the tribes of the earth will mourn, and they will see the Son of Man coming on the clouds of heaven with power and great glory. (Matthew 24:30)

Our responsibility is to be aware, ready, and watchful for the coming of the Lord, Judge, and King. He will come in "power" to judge. He will come in "glory" to be exalted as King and sit on His throne. Praise God! Praise the Exalted One, Jesus! It is essential to read Matthew 24 and 25 to be aware of Christ's coming and be ready as we anticipate His coming soon! Amen and Amen!

King Jesus as Glorious!

> When the Son of man shall come in His glory and all the holy angels with Him. (Matthew 25:31; see also Daniel 7:9–10; Jude 1:14; Hebrews 1:6–7; 1 Peter 3:22)

> Then shall He sit upon the throne of His glory. (Matthew 25:31)

As King, Jesus is finishing all His judgments on the rebellious and sinful people of the world. It will only be those "sheep," those people who have responded to His voice, who will be ushered into His Kingdom as true believers and saints (John 10:27).

The Davidic Covenant that God made with King David stated that a promised descendent would be on the throne. Jesus Christ, the Lord, was the fulfillment of the Davidic Covenant. Our Savior Jesus is in the genealogical line from David, which came to the legal stepfather, Joseph (Matthew 1:20), and His mother Mary (Luke 1:31–32).

> The Lord God will give Him the throne of His father, David. And He will reign over the house of Jacob forever, and of His Kingdom will be no end. (Luke 1:32–33)

God gave the promise from the prophet Nathan to King David in 2 Samuel 7:12–16: "I (God) will set up your seed after you, who will come from your body, and I will establish His Kingdom forever."

Further reassurance is given in Psalm 89:3–4, 35–37 to this covenant in which God has sworn the continued legacy of David's throne to all generations. Yes, Jesus, the rightful King, will be that seed of David to have an everlasting dominion. It will be established as His glorious throne forever and ever. For all of us right now, He is worthy as the Son of David to receive glory, honor, and majesty, as we read in the book of Revelation.

Jesus, Worthy of Adoration

> After these things I heard a loud voice of a great multitude in heaven saying "Alleluia!" Salvation and glory and honor and power belong to the Lord our God! (Revelation 19:1)

Revelation 4–5 also give praise and glory, with shouts of "Alleluia!" repeatedly.

> Worthy is the Lamb who was slain to receive power
> and riches and wisdom, and strength and honor and
> glory and blessing ... Blessing and honor and glory
> and power be to Him who sits on the throne, and
> to the Lamb, forever and ever! (Revelation 5:12–13)

These marvelous verses mentioned will be proclaimed by us, the Church saints, who are glorified and prepared for the inauguration of the King. The Lamb, who was slain, and now entering His Kingdom will hear these praises, blessings, and alleluias. He is a worthy and royal King. Oh, what a sight to behold, so spectacular and glorious!

What else can we say but to reveal what will be portrayed by these scriptures and to look forward to meeting our Lord Jesus in the air? We will return with Christ when He is ready to rule and reign in His Kingdom:

> But at evening time it shall happen that it will be
> light. (Zechariah 14:6–7). The glory and majesty of
> the crowned King Jesus will illumine the events of
> the Marriage Supper of the Lamb.

Christ's Victory over Death

Earlier, we spoke about the resurrection of the dead (1 Corinthians 15). Christ's resurrection gives us the hope of victory as believers also to have glorified bodies and eternal life forever. In 1 Corinthians 15:23ff, there is a resurrection at His coming for the Tribulation saints and Old Testament saints.

> Then comes the end, when He delivers the kingdom
> to God the Father, when He puts an end to all
> rule and all authority and power. (1 Corinthians
> 15:24ff)

Before there is tranquility at the beginning of the Millennial Kingdom, all of Christ's enemies will be judged and removed. He introduces peace as He reigns and rules over His Kingdom. Before He is crowned King at the opening of the Millennium, He has already taken care of all the evil in the world. He has Satan cast in the bottomless pit, so he cannot disturb His reign on the earth (Revelation 20:1–3) Praise the Lord!

> For He must reign till He has put all enemies under
> His feet. The last enemy that will be destroyed is
> death. (1 Corinthians 15:25–26)

The second death (the final death and separation from God) will come by the casting of unbelievers into the lake of fire after the Great White Throne Judgment (Revelation 20:10–15). Even Satan will finally be cast into the lake of fire for his final judgment (v. 10). All who are not in the Book of Life will be cast into the lake of fire. Jesus will put all enemies under His feet. We can rejoice in the truth of Philippians 2:10:

> That at the name of Jesus every knee should bow,
> of those in heaven, and those on earth, and of those
> under the earth.

Our Savior and Lord is worthy to reign in our lives now and forever. When He sets foot on the earth and brings His angels and saints with Him, He will deal with His enemies in judgment and will rightfully sit on His throne in Zion. Is that not exciting?

Jesus Christ, our Lord, probably will not sit down on His rightful throne in Jerusalem until He takes care of the judgment of the evil ones and sinners. At that juncture, He can celebrate with His Bride and saints at the Marriage Feast of the Lamb. Then, and only then, can He be officially inaugurated as the King of His Millennial Kingdom. Can you get this point about Christ finally doing away with evil, corruption, politics, the "evil one," imposters, and the nations that would not follow Him in righteousness? We can say, "With God, all of these prophecies will undeniably come true"!

Also, there is another factor in this transition of days in completing the last three and a half Tribulation years and judgments that must come on the world and God's enemies. It is a gap or allowance of the full reign and blessing of the kingdom for "rest and will arise to your inheritance at the end of the days" (Daniel 12:13).

From the abomination of desolation at the halfway point of the Tribulation to the very end of the Armageddon war, there are 1,290 days (Daniel 12:11). Daniel 12:12 speaks of another forty-five days added:

> Blessed is he who waits, and comes to the one thousand three hundred and thirty-five days. But go your way till the end; for you shall rest. (Daniel 12:12–13)

There is sufficient time for Christ to get all these judgments over before He takes full reign of His Kingdom. It just makes good sense of literal interpretation to fit all this together in one package of time and events. Then we will have the awaited "rest" for the saints. We will rule and reign with the King on His throne. Again, let us just praise the Lord!

And who is counting anyway? Does it matter that us Church saints, the Bride, wait for the Marriage Supper of the Lamb reception? Time will not mean as much to us then as it does now with our watches, cellphone beeps, or wake-up calls in the morning for scheduled appointments. Jesus will be the King worthy of our worship all the time. We will rest in His grace and mercy, and worship will not be a chore or duty as we serve Him at His bidding. The reception of the Bride (the Church) and Groom (Jesus) will be drawn out for days, for all of us to enjoy the food, fellowship, and blessing of being with our Savior King forever. There will always be surprises and the awesomeness of His radiance!

CHAPTER 10

RULING AND REIGNING WITH THE KING JESUS

Then to Him was given dominion and glory and a kingdom,
that all peoples, nations, and languages should serve Him. His
dominion is an everlasting dominion, which shall not pass
away, and His Kingdom the one which shall not be destroyed.
—Daniel 7:14

The Ruling and Reigning with King Jesus

We will count it all joy to be with the "King of kings and Lord of lords" (Revelation 19:16). It says in the parable of the "talents" (Matthew 25) that every good and faithful servant of the Lord would "enter into the joy of your Lord" (Matthew 25:21b).

Oswald J. Smith wrote the words of a meaningful hymn: "There is Joy in Serving Jesus." Indeed, it is a joy to live and serve the Lord of lords and King of kings. Whatever pains, sorrows, and hurts we feel now "will be just a little passing in the night" compared to the glories and glimmering radiance of Christ when He says, "Well done, good and faithful servant" (Matthew 25:21a). Our future reward is to see

Jesus and what He has prepared for us to rule and reign with Him in His glorious kingdom.

The Kingdom to Come

Dr. Timothy Paul Jones states about the glorious kingdom to come:

> What really makes up a potential "Kingdom"? There are three "R's" in an actual Kingdom to come. First, there is the 'Ruler' Jesus. Secondly, the 'Realm' of His domain. And thirdly, the 'Reign' of the everlasting Kingdom. Jesus is the rightful King to rule and reign over His Kingdom.[43]

For us who are of the *Church Age*, also known as the *age of grace*, we have calm assurance in the phrase: "And so we will be with the Lord forever" (1 Thessalonians 4:17 NIV84). Praise God for His promise to come back to take us up in the Rapture to our heavenly home. It will not be too long to wait before He fulfills His promise for us to return later with Him on earth for His Millennial Kingdom.

The Reigning with Jesus

Paul wrote for all genuine Christians to look forward to the day of Christ Jesus the King to return. In so doing, we will be watchful and endure what He has planned for us to do. He said that we who will endure would rule and reign with Him.

> If we endure, we shall also reign with Him. (2 Timothy 2:12)

The Believer's Bible Commentary, by Dr. W. MacDonald and Dr. A. Farstad, explains this verse:

> True faith always has the quality of permanence, and in this sense, all believers will be willing to "endure." He continues to express the truth of this reigning with Christ by saying that "not all will reign with Christ to the same extent. When He comes back to reign over the earth, His saints will return with Him and share in that rule. But the extent of one's rule will be determined by his faithfulness during this present life and time."[44]

Dr. Jamieson also sheds some light on the meaning of this verse.

> The word … "suffer" rather, as the Greek is the same as in 2 Timothy 2:10, with Paul saying, "I endure all things for the sake of the elect …" Thus, "If we endure (with Jesus)" v. 12; and (Romans 8:17) now; "we shall reign with Him" in the future. It is the peculiar privilege of the elect Church who now may suffer in service with Christ, and then later to reign with Him (see 1 Corinthians 6:2). Reigning is something more than mere salvation (Romans 5:17; Revelation 3:21; 5:10). It will be glorious to perform what the King asks of us to do under His rule and reign from Zion.[45]

The Ruling with Jesus

Those raptured will come and reign with Christ Jesus the King:

We who are alive and remain shall be caught up together with them (just seconds after the dead are raised) in the clouds to meet the Lord in the air. (1 Thessalonians 4:13–18)

These are the firstfruits of those like Jesus who rose from the dead and ever lives for us in heaven. Dr. MacDonald and Dr. Farstad write:

> "There is the implication that Paul wrote to Timothy of a faithful saying that these Church saints 'endure'; will also 'reign with Him, if we deny Him, He also will deny us' (2 Timothy 2:12). In a sense, it is also true of all Christians that as they endure now, then they will also reign with Christ. True faith always has the quality of permanence, and in this sense, all believers do" endure" until the day Christ calls us to be with Him forever. …. "not all will reign with Christ to the same extent." But the scope of one's rule will be determined by his faithfulness during this present life."[46]

A Realm of being Priests

In Revelation 5:9–12, we read that the Church saints are priests:

> You have redeemed us to God by Your blood … and have made us kings and priests to our God; and we shall reign on the earth. (See also Revelation 20:6, "priests of God.")

First Peter 2:9a, emphasizes this as well: "You are a chosen generation, a royal priesthood." It seems probable that our priestly duties continue with King Jesus, who may have us in positions as mediating priests of people on earth to His throne room. Dr. Walvoord and Dr. Zuck said:

> As the KJV states and we believe that it is correct, the 24 elders must represent the Church or saints in general. It would seem most definitely, that since the elders are on thrones and are crowned as victors, they represent the Church. Yes, and praise the Lord, angels do join the living creatures and the elders in praising the Lamb (Revelation 5:11–12).
>
> For hundreds of years, God's people have been praying for the return of Christ and the righting of wrongs in the world. One day surely, God will answer those prayers. "We shall reign on earth" (5:10) is their expectation. This is another proof that Christ will one day reign over a literal kingdom on earth. See Revelation 20:4.[47]

The twenty-four elders in the book of Revelation are the representatives of the Church Age saints returning with Christ Jesus in the defeat at Armageddon. They will be coming from heaven with King Jesus on white horses, dressed in fine white linen to accompany Christ as a host of an army (Revelation 19:14). Yet, Jesus alone will defeat the enemy and its leaders to set these saints in capacities of duties at the outset of the Millennium.

The Resurrection and Reward of the Martyrs

John recorded in Revelation 20:4–6 that there is another set of thrones. Those who have the authority to judge are seated on those thrones. Besides, he "saw the souls of those who had been beheaded"

(Revelation 20:4). They were those who stood true to the Lord and His Word during the Great Tribulation. The fact that John could see them implies that they had received intermediate bodies in heaven and were awaiting their resurrection.

The Tribulation Saints

> And I saw thrones, and they sat on them, and judgment was committed to them. Then I saw the souls of those who had been beheaded for their witness to Jesus and for the word of God, who had not worshiped the beast or his image, and had not received his mark on their foreheads or on their hands. (Revelation 20:4)

John the apostle saw, in his apocalyptic writings of the Revelation, a sight of more authoritative thrones. These people will be beheaded for the witness and testimony they had of the "Word of God" and Jesus in their hearts. These believers will not take the mark of "666" of the Antichrist "beast" during the seven-year Tribulation period after the Rapture of the Church saints (Revelation 13:18). The Antichrist will be the beast that comes out of the sea (13:1). This group of saints who trusted Jesus as their personal Savior will make the ultimate sacrifice (being beheaded). They will trust Jesus as their Lord and won't submit to the world's dictator's whims and wishes. They will refuse to worship his image and will be beheaded for their faith (v. 15).

This band of martyred Tribulation saints will enter the Millennial Kingdom in resurrected bodies like any of the Church saints who are raptured. They are rewarded by having thrones and dominion ranks. Revelation 20:4 says that they "lived and reigned with Christ for a thousand years." They will have all the rights and privileges as the Church saints, yet possibly not have the crowns that will be given at the "Judgment Seat of Christ" (2 Corinthians 5:10). Nothing is mentioned of these heroic saints having a similar bema-type recognition, yet it is just understood they have thrones to reign with Christ.

Revelation 20:5 and 6 are very hard verses to interpret. The phrase "the first resurrection" is mentioned twice. "The first resurrection" in verse six refers to all the bodily resurrections from the Rapture of the Church saints to the Tribulation saints who will be ruling and reigning with Christ in the Millennium. Revelation 20:7 goes directly into the judgment of the "Great White Throne" which is after "the thousand years have expired" (vv. 6–7). Dr. Warren Wiersbe says:

> The first part of Revelation 20:5, must be understood as a parenthesis. The rest of the dead refers to unbelievers of all ages who will be raised at the end of the Millennium to stand before the Judgment of the Great White Throne. All who are raised in the first resurrection are saved people; they will not experience the second death, which is hell. See John 5:24–29.[48]

Those of the First Resurrection

Revelation 20:4–6 talks about those of the first Resurrection. *The Believer's Bible Commentary* gives a list of the various resurrection occurrences:

> The statement "this is the first resurrection," refers back to verse 4. The first resurrection is not a single event. It describes the resurrection of the righteous at various times. It includes the resurrection of Christ (1 Corinthians 15:23), the resurrection

of those who are Christ's when He raptures the Church (1 Thessalonians 4:13–18), the resurrection of the two witnesses whose bodies will lie in the streets (Revelation 11:11), and the resurrection of Tribulation saints who are described here (see also Daniel 12:2a). In other words, the first resurrection includes the resurrection of Christ and of all true believers, though they are raised at different times. It occurs in several stages of the revelation of such.[49]

The Old Testament Saints

Of course, we cannot forget that the Old Testament saints will be there in Christ's kingdom. Jesus will set them up in a ruling capacity near Himself in Zion. The twelve tribes of Jacob will have their inheritance in dividing up the Promised Land from the Gaza Peninsula to the north and east to the Euphrates River. The scriptures say that the landmass and extension of the tribes will exceed what King David and Solomon had conquered in their lifetime (Ezekiel 47:13– 48:29).

The "How" of the Saints Ruling and Reigning

We, as God's saved saints, will be ruling, judging, and reigning with Christ in His glorious kingdom. I am happy to share from the scriptures what Jesus and others have said about this first resurrection of God's elect to serve and rule with Christ Jesus the King.

Like Christ's Glorified Body

> When He is revealed, we shall be like Him, for we
> shall see Him as He is. (1 John 3:2)

How shall we be like the resurrected Lord Jesus? When Christ rose from the dead and the grave, He could walk through walls and appear and disappear with His resurrected body. If you remember the two Sundays where the eleven disciples were in the upper room with the door closed, Jesus said, "Peace be unto you" (Luke 24:36). The disciples were startled with excitement. Just think, if we are like Jesus in His resurrected, glorified body, we will also be able to appear and disappear. We may float or fly around the countryside, performing what King Jesus commands for us to do from His throne in Zion.

Christ's Travels

Let me explain the forty days of Christ's movement after His resurrection. Biblical scholars tell us that in Emmaus when Jesus ate with Cleopas and another disciple, He had just walked with them from Jerusalem. Jesus had sat down with them at their supper table when "He vanished from their sight" (Luke 24:31) or "disappeared from their sight" (NIV84). Jesus just departed from their fellowship around the dining table. These men's hearts burned within them because they were just with the resurrected Savior. These circumstances were so amazing to them that they ran back nine kilometers to Jerusalem to climb up the stairs into the upper room that first Easter night.

Where did Jesus go after telling Mary Magdalene not to cling to Him in the garden near the tomb in John 20:17? Jesus said He had not returned to His Father yet. Jesus said to Mary, "Do not cling to Me, for I have not yet ascended to My Father" (v. 17). Did Jesus go to His Father that first resurrection morning after being with Mary in the garden?

The verse seems to say so! Could Jesus ascend to the highest heaven and come immediately back to earth again to walk with the two men to Emmaus? Yes, He could if He wanted to! Did He go to the captives in hell to share that He was victorious over death and the grave? What was his purpose in going to the lost souls in hell? Was it to explain that God's plan of salvation was missed out on by their refusal to believe in Him as their Lord and Savior (Ephesians 4:9–10; 1 Peter 1:19–20)? Some commentators put this descent as happening between Christ's death and resurrection, but the event could be after the Resurrection since that first Easter morn was supremely victorious. The descent could have been between the late hours of the resurrection Sunday morning and His joining the two men on the road to Emmaus (Luke 24:15–16). These reasons are all speculation. How could we have sufficient salvation without a risen Savior? Praise the Lord; "He has risen!"

Then we have the possibility of Jesus visiting with His half-brothers, half-sisters, and Mary, His mother (proof of the family: Matthew 13:55–56). We find that James, Jesus's half-brother, was a believer after Jesus rose from the grave. He personally saw Jesus's glorified resurrected body (1 Corinthians 15:7). Jesus must have shown his scarred, pierced hands and glorified body to his oldest half-brother who had been most skeptical of Jesus up until that time. It was at that time after Jesus's resurrection that James believed Jesus was the very divine Son of God. Possibly Mary had told her family that she saw her Son, Jesus, nailed to the cross. This James became the pastor of the Jerusalem church in the months and years to come (Galatians 1:19). All these appearances and happenings proved that Jesus could travel about without walking or riding a mule. He was able to walk through walls and disappear and appear in various places to show people that He is Lord.

Believer's Glorified Bodies

At Jesus's Second Advent to return to the earth, we who have been like Him will have similar glorified bodies (1 John 3:2). It will be most likely that we will also be able to fly around and disappear and appear. He wants us to rule and reign for Him around the world. We will be able to take flight without wings and get to New York City, Tokyo, Frankfurt, or London in a minute or less. We will be Christ's spokespersons in places of the world and fly back to Jerusalem to get instructions, take seminars, or just worship the King in honor and majesty.

Is that not amazing that the King wants us saints to assist Him and get back with Him at His throne? We will rule and reign with Him all over the world in a peaceful, loving, miraculous, and prosperous Millennial Kingdom. Praise and honor be to the King! Flesh and blood people in the Millennium will be surprised when we can vanish out of their sight, appear, and disappear whenever needed. We will deliver the words of "Peace be unto you" (Luke 24:36 NIV84) from the King of kings! We will have our designated regions of the world to minister in, as the King will give us clear responsibility. We will supervise the flesh-and-blood families and construction sites in the Millennium. We will be following the King's mandates in serving and honoring Him. Some will be startled and amazed, to say the least, as the ten disciples were when Jesus surprised them by showing up that first Easter night in the upper room (Luke 24:37).

The "Where" of All These Saints Ruling and Reigning

Jesus taught His disciples some of the happenings and preparations for the millennial reign of His Kingdom. In Matthew 25, Jesus taught in His sermon on the Mount of Olives that we as His followers should be "watchful" for we "know neither the day or the hour in which the Son of Man is coming" (Matthew 25:13). The parable Jesus told was that there were ten virgins similar to bridesmaids who were waiting for the groom to come for the wedding. He was late coming, yet there were five who still had sufficient oil in their lamps. They could take part in the wedding ceremony. Jesus's point was to commend the wise maidens who brought enough oil for the long wait until the bridegroom showed himself to the bride and loved ones. We are to be on the alert, prepared, and watchful until the coming of our Lord Jesus.

"Well Done" Servants

The next parable Jesus told was the "parable of the talents" (Matthew 25:14–30; Luke 19:12–27). Read both passages to see the relationship between the awards and reigning with Christ in the Millennium. Maybe you know the story. A nobleman (representing Jesus Himself) would be going away into a far country to receive a kingdom. Usually, at the time of Jesus, the Roman emperor would designate a particular region for a nobleman to rule. The man of great wealth and prestige in the parable left his servants a sizeable weight of money. The servants were to do business until he returned.

When the master returned, he called the servants and asked for an accounting of their management of the funds he had given them. The servant who received five talents traded to make another five talents. The servant who received two talents, likewise, gained two other talents. Their master praised both men:

> Well done, good and faithful servant; you were faithful over a few things, I will make you ruler over many things. Enter into the joy of your lord. (Matthew 25:21)

They awarded two of the three servants a "well done" commendation for their service to their master, and the third servant was reprimanded.

Rewards for the Servants

The Lord Jesus, the King, will be faithful to reward our diligence here on earth while He is away at this time in heaven. He will return to reward us who are His servants with responsibilities and duties in His Millennial Kingdom. The Luke passage says that the one who gained the ten minas would receive the authority to be governor over ten cities (Luke 19:18). Likewise, the one who gained five pounds or minas would be ruling over five cities in Christ's Millennial Kingdom. It is wonderful to know that we will, in our glorified bodies, reign over so many cities in the world. With those responsibilities, we will get our authority from the King of kings Himself to rule and reign. We will be going forth from Jerusalem to our designated provinces and from Jerusalem to make wise decisions from the Master's perspective. Glory be to the King of kings who reigns over the whole world in this theocratic government.

So, where do you want to rule and reign in service with King Jesus in His Millennium? Is it in the Philippines, the United States, China, Africa, Canada, Central or South America, Europe, or Asia? You just put in your request, and you may be surprised that Jesus may give you "the desire of your heart" (Psalm 37:4).

May we be prepared and know that what we do now in this Church Age of our lifetime here before the Rapture will be awarded later at the Bema Seat of Christ (2 Corinthians 5:10). His judgment verdict will be with many rewards or none. The loss of reward (in the realm of "wood, hay, and straw") means any beneficial rewards God would like to give will be burned up and just vanish (1 Corinthians 3:12–15). At the Bema Seat, we will know how we will rule with Him for a thousand years in Christ Jesus's kingdom. It will be the time to receive jewels in our crowns, which will give us the authority to govern for King Jesus in various parts of the world (1 Corinthians 3:12–13; 2 Timothy 4:8).

CHAPTER 11

THE PEACEFUL RULE OF CHRIST THE KING IN THE MILLENNIUM

My people will dwell in a peaceful habitation, in
secure dwellings, and in quiet resting places.
—Isaiah 32:18

Prince of Peace: Ruling from His Throne

I saiah describes Jesus as the "Wonderful Counselor, Mighty
God ... Prince of Peace" (Isaiah 9:6). Verse 7 adds this phrase:
"Of the increase of His government and peace, there is no
end; upon the throne of David and over His Kingdom." Yes, He
is the Prince, highly favored and royal in His dignity and divinity.
He came in His First Advent by the birth of a lowly state, and His
life and ministry were that of a humble Nazarene, meek and lowly
(Matthew 2:23). He even rode a donkey into Jerusalem (John 12:14).
Jesus brought forth peace in His life and death for our salvation
(Isaiah 53:5; Romans 5:1). Jesus said, "My peace I give to you; not
as the world gives do I give to you" (John 14:27). Jesus has so many
aspects of being the "Prince of Peace" in His First Advent, and now
we speak of Him making peace in His Second Advent.

Even from the beginning of the prophet Isaiah's prophecies,

there is coming a time in the latter days that Jesus will reign from the Holy Mount of Jerusalem as the capital of His kingship (Isaiah 2:2–4). His Kingdom will be inaugurated and established. He will rule from Jerusalem, a place of worship for the nations to come to Him and give allegiance to the King of kings. For out of Zion (Jerusalem) will come His teaching and principles to live by. What He says He will do. He will teach His representatives. There will be "on earth peace, goodwill toward men" (Luke 2:14). Jesus will judge between nations peacefully, and no one will take up arms against each other. It will be a time of peace and no war. There will be no studying about war (Isaiah 2:4; Micah 4:3), and no one will rebel against Christ. God will break up any thoughts or opposition against His theocratic (God and only God ruling) peaceful government.

No More War

We could conclude from Isaiah 2:4 and Micah 4:3 that there will be no more war factories for implements of guns, missiles, bombs, bullets, tanks, or military aircraft. There will be no soldiers to keep the peace in protecting a nation. There will be no war. Christ will put an end to all armies at the final Armageddon battle. Personal arms and military weapons will be turned in and melted down for recycled machinery to rebuild the world. Tribulation trauma and devastation will turn into beautiful, green earth.

The genuine believers with flesh-and-blood bodies from the seven-year Tribulation will enter these thousand years of worship to the King Jesus. The world will be calm and peaceful compared to the chaos of the Tribulation period. Ezekiel 39:7–10 tells us that, if need be, for seven years into the Millennium, war paraphernalia will be disarmed and used to make new steel building supplies and machinery such as cranes, trucks, bulldozers, earthmovers, and similar equipment for peaceful communities. "Nations shall not lift up sword against nation; neither shall they learn war anymore" (Isaiah 2:4b).

Praise God there will be no more war in the millennial reign of Christ. There will be no more war colleges, military camps, barracks, colonels, generals, or sergeants to teach soldiers how to fight against an enemy. Christ Jesus the King will make "on earth peace, goodwill toward men" (Luke 2:14).

The Peace That Will Prevail

Rather than the turmoil of war (Amos 2:13–16; 3:11; 4:10–11; 5:2–3; 9:1, 10), there will be unbroken peace which will enable Israel to enjoy the fruit of her labor (Leviticus 26:6–8; Deuteronomy 28:6–10). This Kingdom age will be the most marvelous, quiet, and tranquil time on earth since the Garden of Eden.

Even during the Cold War, men made peace treaties, but they all failed. The Antichrist's future peace treaty during the first part of the Tribulation years will also fail. Even Jesus's First Advent brought divisions and fighting and not peace. Jesus stated in Matthew 10:21, 34–36: "Do not think that I came to bring peace on earth. I did not come to bring peace but a sword. For I have come to 'set a man against his father, a daughter against her mother, and a daughter-in-law against her mother-in-law; and a man's enemies will be those of his household." (We also see this idea in Micah 7:6). Are these kinds of troubles and disputes happening all around us today? Yes, indeed! There will not be lasting peace until Jesus the King sets up His Millennial Kingdom to come.

Peace and Prosperity in Agricultural Food Production

In this passage of the peaceful domain of Isaiah's prophecies (Isaiah 2:4a), Jesus will "judge between the nations and rebuke many people; they shall beat their swords into plowshares and their spears into pruning hooks." These circumstances and transitions into the Millennium will ensure that any war apparatus will be made into peaceful agricultural tractors, plows, discs, cultivators, corn planters, and harvesters. The scriptures say that while swords (guns) were used in wartime, they will now be made into plows, and the tips of the spears (bullets) of war will be made into pruning hooks or knives that would trim and cut vines. Jesus illustrated this in John 15. The context is that the heavenly Father will prune off (shorten) those branches (of our trials and problems); while we abide with Christ now, we will produce abundant, obedient fruit in maturity. God will help His children to become more like the Lord Jesus Christ. A question for all of us is this: Are we producing fruit that will last and mature in our lives to be pleasing to the Lord God?

The Agricultural Development

Since there will be no more war, agricultural development will expand to produce more food for the needs of a growing population during the Millennium. Micah 4:2 mentions, as Isaiah did, that Jesus will reign from Zion. His Law and Word will be strong, and He will rule mightily. He will judge many peoples throughout the world. He will rebuke strong nations that want to war against Him.

Accordingly, the weapons of war will be recycled into "plowshares" and the spears into "pruning hooks." These "hooks" are agricultural trimming scissors that can cut back the branches of the fruit trees to bear more healthy fruit for all seasons, which is mentioned so many times in Ezekiel 47. Organic fruits and vegetables will continue to be researched and provide enriched natural methods of safe products for all people to enjoy without the effects of chemical spray and enhancements.

You may want to look up Ezekiel 47:6–12 to understand the importance of a river flowing with fruit trees along its banks, yielding fruit all the months of the year (v. 12). The river we are talking about is the one upon which Jesus will touch down with His feet on Mount Olives (Zechariah 14:4). The mountain will split, and water will flow out east and west (v. 8). The water that flows east, as described by Ezekiel, will come from the sanctuary of God in Jerusalem, which will be a source of healing that will revive the Dead Sea. The Dead Sea will have a thriving fishing industry with fertilizer along its inlets and swamps (47:8–11). The river itself—with its irrigation canals, fruit trees, vegetables, and the like—will have herbs that will be processed into medicines during this millennial reign of Christ (Ezekiel 47:12).

The Prince to Control Peace

One day, I asked a fellow professor at our Bible college in the Philippines, "Which place will be more spectacular—the present heaven or the Millennium?" He had heard so much about the Millennium in his seminary master's program that he exalted the Millennium over the heaven of those who are "absent from the body present with the Lord" (2 Corinthians 5:8.9). Even though I had given a glamorous outlook for the Millennium, we need to realize that there will be people living (with flesh and blood bodies) who will act contrary to the King. At the end of the Millennium, these children of the saved Tribulation believers will rebel when God lets Satan loose to deceive the nations. Sin and acts of sins will still be evident in the Millennium, but in the present heaven described by the Bible and in the presence of God, there will be no sin. In the Millennium, there will be sin exposed and dealt with by King Jesus during His reign here. I concluded that heaven now would be much more holy and especially spectacular because God is there—and no rebellious sin is taking place.

The Healing from the Prince of Peace

I also asked my friend, "At the end of the Tribulation, what will happen to believers who are sick with cancer or other serious diseases? Will they still have to go through chemotherapy?"

My friend very quickly said that this King Jesus, the great Physician, will heal all diseases in making everything new, enduring, and in peaceful existence, at least at the beginning of the Millennium. If at His First Advent as "Emmanuel" on earth, Jesus healed all types of diseases, so too in His presence at His inauguration, the Marriage Feast of the Lamb, He will make all things new. Honor and glory go to Him! He will give wisdom and knowledge to medical professionals to have healing in all roots, fruits, and leaves of plant life (Ezekiel 47:12). It will be so exciting to think about this future Millennium! Praise be to the God of gods!

Joy and Peace

Isaiah 65–66 is full of references to the joy in Jerusalem. God wants His believing loved ones to rejoice in what He will do for His selected city:

> But be glad and rejoice forever in what I create; for behold, I create Jerusalem as a rejoicing and her people a joy ... I will rejoice in Jerusalem, and joy in My people. (Isaiah 65:18)

> Behold, I will extend peace to her like a river, and the glory of the Gentiles like a flowing stream, then you shall feed; On her sides shall you be carried. (Isaiah 66:12)

The peace given from Christ Jesus the King is like a tranquil river. Even Gentiles will enjoy the peace and joy of the King's presence in Zion. A literal river is shown in scripture to be an actual flowing river of life, which will bring abundant organic healing. Ezekiel 47:12 says of the trees along the bank of the river, "Their fruit will be for food, and their leaves for medicine." We who are saints in our glorified bodies will see those who will be alive and well physically, rejoicing in God and the King, who will be making everything new, abundant, beautiful, and prosperous for living on the earth in this Millennial Kingdom.

Food in Abundance for All to Enjoy the Life as God Meant It to Be

A River of Life

God's special flowing water will be real and pure from His abundance in nourishing the fertile green earth. The actual river, which comes from God's sanctuary (the Millennial Temple), will have abundant enriching springs of living water that bring irrigation, gardens, and orchards of fruit (Ezekiel 47). It will have all kinds of fruit trees and medicinal aspects of leaves, bark, and roots that will help in the longevity of life. This river itself will pass down to the Jordan Valley. According to Isaiah 66:12, people "shall feed on her sides" (the fruit of its trees and irrigated gardens). I speculate that there may be larger than usual numerical families (of people who have flesh and blood), as people may live to be two or three hundred years old.

In Isaiah, we read that children will live long lives. It is almost a pity if they do not live for a hundred years:

> No more shall an infant from there live for a few
> days, nor an old man who has not fulfilled his days;

for the child shall die one hundred years old, but also the sinner being one hundred years old shall be accursed; they shall build houses and inhabit them; they shall plant vineyards and eat their fruit. (Isaiah 65:20–21)

Do you want to live a long life and your children after you? They just might live longer than you do. Do you understand the thought and interpretation here in these verses? If a person dies at age of a hundred, they may still look like a teenager. And those who may be put to death as a criminal sinner at a hundred years old would be cursed and shamed that they could not have lived a full life of two hundred plus years.

How exciting it will be in the Millennium! Some might question how would there be enough food for all these people during the thousand years of the kingdom. Yet, praise God, we find in various scripture passages that the fertile agricultural soil of that time will feed the growing population. Praise the Lord! Aren't you glad God has this all worked out for humanity to be healthy, wealthy, and wise? I am especially looking forward to that time when the agronomy (agribusiness) farming and agriculture during the Millennium will feed all the people, and I can also enjoy some tasty fruits and vegetables.

The Harvest Will Be Abundant

We have already discussed the turnover of all guns and weapons of mass destruction. There will be no more war or soldiers. Many will become farmers to feed all the billions of people alive by the end of the millennial time of Christ's reign as King:

"Behold, the days are coming," says the LORD, "when the plowman shall overtake the reaper, and the treader of grapes him who sows seed; the mountains shall drip with sweet wine, and all the hills shall flow with it. I will bring back the captives of My people Israel; they shall build the waste cities and inhabit them; they shall plant vineyards and drink wine from them; they shall also make gardens and eat fruit from them. I will plant them in their land, and no longer shall they be pulled up from the land I have given them." (Amos 9:13–15)

Fruits and vegetables will be in abundance!

Modern Techniques

Can you imagine? Whether you know much about gardening, vineyards, orchards, or farming, the abundance of yield and harvest during the Millennium will be amazing. It will be a super yield in what farmers will gain in their crops. The above verses state that after the harvest is in, the modern threshing machines will come back to the barn, and quickly, the tractor drivers will want to go out to prepare the ground to cultivate the fields again for planting. These tractor drivers will get anxious to get on the fields and say, "When is the last day of your harvest so we can plow again?" There will not be a fallow time of waiting before planting the next crop. Corn can be planted quickly again over the same field they may have just harvested. Yes, the agriculturalists will be busy teaching crop rotation then as they do now for some preservation of the soils and getting a good yield on many of the various grain harvests and vegetable farming.

Vineyards in Abundance

Amos 9 says that grapes will be abundant in various varieties. At the harvest time in Israel and neighboring countries, grapes will be dripping with juice (v. 13). The ground will be covered so much that it may even run down the rows or roads with the purple liquid grape juice. Assuredly, the smell of grapes will be in the air. And of course, they will try to harvest the grapes before they start dripping down the hillsides as described in these verses. God is good all the time!

My wife and I know one young missionary lady who went to Israel to pick grapes by hand. The delicate varieties of grapes that are exported or eaten fresh must be selected by hand and carefully packed for shipping and selling in the marketplace. Yet, even now, there are modern equipment as grape pickers, mounted on a tractor that are self-propelled on tall wheels to harvest grapes used for grape juice or wine. I have seen these machines harvesting the grapes that are near our place in western New York. They use these grapes for Welsh's grape juice, jellies, jams, and candies. Yum!

My dad was an average, everyday sort of farmer. The Lord blessed abundantly what my father planted and raised on his small farm. He had four cows, calves, and chickens as his livestock. His philosophy for fruits and vegetables was to prepare the soil, plant the seeds, and trim the fruit trees to produce what God intended him to harvest. God was gracious in whatever the climate, rain, heat of the sun, and outcome would yield. We, as a family, would do our best to sell the harvest of produce and preserve much for the winter months. God was exceptionally gracious to my parents in that way—even without irrigation or springs of flowing water coming by our farm. We praised God, and He provided the increase and support of the family.

The technology of today's big business farmers will carry over to the Millennium. I shared about the hard work and sweat that farmers have had since the beginning (going back to Genesis 3, concerning the curse). But humans have improved since the days of using domestic animals of oxen, teams of horses, and mules to do the plowing and cultivation. Modern large tractors may not even use plows anymore; instead, chisel plows make a wider path in the earth. Some tractors plant vegetables in straight rows with GPS satellite gauges in their cabs. It also calculates how many kilos of seeds are necessary per acre of cultivated farmland. This kind of technology will most likely continue in the Millennium with more precision than what we have in the twenty-first century.

Deserts Turned into Fertile Production

Most definitely, in the days when God restores Israel, the land will be very productive with an abundance of food (Isaiah 27:6).

> And it will come to pass in that day, that the mountains shall drip with new wine, the hills shall flow with milk, and all the brooks of Judah shall be flooded with water; a fountain shall flow from the house of the LORD. (Joel 3:18)

> The wilderness and the wasteland shall be glad for them, and the desert shall rejoice and blossom as the rose; it shall blossom abundantly and rejoice, even with joy and singing. (Isaiah 35:1–2)

Again, this shows God's abundant provisions of food and wine for His Kingdom. People will enjoy the production of food for the multiplying population. The grapes will hang so heavy in the mountain vineyards that the hills will drip and flow with vats overflowing, and the hillsides will appear from a distance to be "dissolving" as softened purple mud oozes down the slopes.

God's restored people, Israel, will live in peace and be able to enjoy lavish abundance. The frustration and insecurity of war will be a thing of the past (Isaiah 2:4: Micah 4:3). They will build houses and even whole cities and live in them (Isaiah 32:18). There will be rejoicing with abundance and enjoyment of food and fellowship at parties. Like we said earlier, people like to eat and talk of all the goodness and glory of God.

Dr. Warren Wiersbe adds, "Amos closes his prophecies on a note of victory, for in 9:11–15 we have the promise of the future restoration of God's chosen Israel. Verses eleven and twelve are quoted in Acts 15:14–18 at the first church conference."[50]

This church council was held in Jerusalem. James, the first pastor of the Jerusalem church, quoted from this Acts passage:

> So that the rest of mankind may seek the LORD,
> even all the Gentiles who are called by My name;
> says the LORD, who does these things. (Acts 15:17)

God is in control and will do all these marvelous works. Today, God is calling out of the nations, a people for His name, even including the Gentiles. When God completes the Church, He will return and restore the Temple of David and establish His Jewish kingdom (Millennial Kingdom). God's unique land will become fruitful again, prophecies will be fulfilled, and His saints will be blessed forever.

CHAPTER 12

WHO ARE ALL THESE PEOPLE IN THE PRESENCE OF THE KING?

All kings will bow down to Him, and all nations will serve Him.
— Psalm 72:11

The Labor Force during the Millennial Kingdom

The Millennial Kingdom of our Lord will have various groups of people who are all working together under the leadership of Jesus Christ, the King. The days are coming when God will restore covenant blessings to the land of Israel (Leviticus 26:3–10; Deuteronomy 28:1–14; Amos 9:13). There will be everlasting prosperity in Christ's kingdom.

The Gentile Workers

One of the groups of people who labor in the Millennium will be the Gentile workforce. There will be others as well, both Jews and Gentiles. They will be the plowmen, harvesters, drivers of equipment for construction, and builders of cities, as mentioned in the prophecies of old. In Isaiah 61:4–6ff, the context is like the rebuilding and restoration of Israel after the exile from Babylon. A double fulfillment in its totality will be in the Millennium: "They shall rebuild the old ruins; they shall raise up the former desolations" (v. 4). It also states here that the neighboring Gentile strangers will tend their flocks and be their plowmen in the field and vinedressers. The living saved Gentile individuals from the seven-year Tribulation time, who are transferred directly into the Millennium with flesh and blood, will be the typical workforce during this reign of Christ.

Job Superintendents

The reigning and ruling saints, both Jew and Gentile, will have the management duties. They will have the agricultural and building contracts to make a good working relationship between the hierarchy and the common laborers. Christ will reward those glorified saints with positions as mayors, governors, supervisors, and inspectors of the rebuilding process of the Kingdom, whether in Jerusalem or nations around the world (Luke 19:15–19). As the population grows, with extended life and modern technology, there will be a need for workers in agriculture and construction of the Millennium temple, cities, and nations around the entire earth.

The Jewish Leadership

According to scripture, the descendants of Abraham are and always will be the chosen people who God especially blesses. From the early Patriarchs—King David and Jesus—the Jews are in a higher rank of service or leadership than the Gentiles. Yet, the Bible is not fully clear about those Jewish people in management matters of ruling and reigning.

The Isaiah 61 passage states that Jews will benefit from the riches and bounty that the Gentiles will provide.

> But you shall be named the priests of the LORD,
> they shall call you servants of our God. You shall
> eat the riches of the Gentiles, and in their glory, you
> shall boast. (v. 6)

In the "glory" of the Gentile workers, the Jews will "boast."

> The sons of the foreigner will be your plowmen and
> your vinedressers. (v. 5)

Those "foreigners" will be the Gentile race in contrast to the chosen Jewish descendants.

The Bride of Christ: Saints with the Other People of the Kingdom

In the Millennium, a variety of saints will work and serve the King in countless positions. The Bride of Christ saints from the Church Age will receive rewards at the Bema Seat of Christ (2 Corinthians 5:10). They will be the most favored (as the most beloved Groom's wife) of all the past ages as His chosen "body of Christ." These Church saints will include both Jews and Gentiles.

The Jewish saints of all times will always be rewarded a higher status than the Gentile saints, whether they are Tribulation saints or Old Testament saints. The Old Testament Gentile proselytes who were circumcised in keeping with the Law may be equal to the descendants of Abraham. Yet even those proselyte Gentiles may be a lower rank than a full-blooded Jew. All of this is speculation, yet scripture has repeatedly put the priority on the Jewish (Hebrew) people. I conclude that the righteous Jewish person will receive more privileges. God will favor a descendent of Abraham, who has obeyed and lived in an approved relationship with God, over a Gentile.

In Isaiah 61:4–6, we see the benefits of being a true Israelite. God names them as priests of the LORD. The Gentiles will do things for the Jewish people in producing food and wine and constructing beautiful homes, buildings, and landscapes. May the Lord King be honored and glorified!

Crowns for Jesus's Bride

The Bride of Christ will be rewarded with crowns (Revelation 4–5). There are five types of crowns listed in the New Testament: 1}. "the crown of life" (James 1:12; Revelation 2:10), 2}. "the crown of righteousness" (2 Timothy 4:8), 3}. "the unfading crown of glory" (1 Peter 5:4), 4}. "the crown of joy" (1 Thessalonians 2:19), and 5}. "the crown that is imperishable" (1 Corinthians 9:15). These crowns are given in heaven after the Rapture at the Bema Seat of Christ (1 Corinthians 3; 2 Corinthians 5).

These crowned saints will have kingly duties, supervising capacities, and responsibilities given directly by Jesus Christ from His throne in Zion. I believe, as scripture says, that we will be laying our crowns at King Jesus's feet (Revelation 4:10). Jesus will probably place them back on our heads for the positions He has designated to us to rule. Those crowns will show that we have a position of rank over other people in the kingdom and rulers around the world.

Glorified Bodies

The Church Age saints will have resurrected, glorified bodies, as stated in the previous chapters. We will be as Christ was after His resurrection. We will walk through walls, appear, and disappear when traveling and giving orders from the King. When Jesus was in the upper room with His disciples, He mentioned that He was not a spirit (or ghost) but with "flesh and bones." Indeed, the disciples saw Him in His physical appearance (Luke 24:39). We usually think of humans as having "flesh and blood." Our glorified bodies must also have bone structure; even Mary Magdalene could hang on to Jesus's ankles in the garden (John 20:17: Matthew 28:9).

These glorified bodied saints from the age of grace (the Church Age) from Pentecost to the Rapture are distinct in their governing roles. They fly to and from the King's sanctuary throne room to the designated cities, farms, factories, and countries around the world. Do these leadership and oversight responsibilities frighten you? God will give us the wisdom and energy to obey His mandates in keeping a peaceful kingdom. Just think, there you will be with your precious jewels (1 Corinthians 3:12) in your crown and authority to rule and reign with the King of kings, and Lord of lords.

The Tribulation Saints, Who have Endured Even Martyrdom

The main verse about Tribulation saints who have been martyred for Christ is Revelation 20:4. John saw and wrote down here: "And I saw thrones, and they sat on them, and judgment was committed to them." It is expected from the reading the chapters of the book of Revelation that these future Tribulation saints (during the seven years of the Tribulation) will suffer martyrdom and cruelty more than believers in the past. These future saints are special. They are included in responsibilities with authority just as the saints of the Church Age. They have endured the worst of times and escaped the magnitude of persecution (by premature death) during the last years before Christ reveals Himself and defeats all evil.

Saints on Thrones

It says in Revelation 20:4 that these saints "sit on thrones." Thus, these precious Tribulation saints will also have ruling positions in judgment calls as judges, lawyers, counselors, and supervisors possibly alongside the Church saints. These saints are reigning on thrones in their perspective places designated from Christ their King. We consider these future martyrdom saints full of even greater faith than we who have life easier now before the Rapture of the Church. Surely God will include them in the "Hall of Faithful Ones" as in Hebrews 11.

The 144,000 Witnesses

Who are some of these Tribulation saints? We find in the book of Revelation that there will be 144,000 witnesses. They are from the twelve tribes of Israel. Twelve thousand from each tribe do not take on the mark of the beast (Revelation 7:1–8). They preach the Gospel of salvation by grace through faith (Ephesians 2:8–9). They also tell of the kingdom to come where Jesus will return to set up a righteous and plenteous kingdom of a thousand years. If Jesus mandated His would-be followers to preach the kingdom of God in Luke 9:60, how much more when these witnesses are so close to the time of Jesus's Second Advent?

Some of Christ's missionaries will be martyred, beheaded, or just killed at random during the Tribulation time. Recently, we have seen the prelude of beheading that the ISIS movement has done in the Middle East. It is a sign of Jesus's coming.

Two of those Witnesses

Two of these witnesses will be killed and left in the streets for four days and will come alive to be ascended to heaven in glorified bodies (Revelation 11:3–12). They, too, will be a part of these ruling classes of judges and superintendents for the King from Zion. Their reward and blessings will be to look forward to serving the Christ, whom they had served to the point of laying down their lives for Him. This group of people is unique and worthy of having a rulership position in Christ's kingdom.

These Tribulation saints may be different from both Jew and Gentile Christians in that they will receive honor and reward for their steadfast endurance to the end. They will be martyred for Christ and His testimony. These 144,000 witnesses may have a higher reward than the Gentile Christians during the seven-year Tribulation. It is God's sovereign will to prefer these descendants of Abraham over the Gentile Christians. These believing saints seem to be of utmost importance and will be established on thrones to rule and reign with King Jesus (Revelation 20:4).

Surely it will be great when God presents to all the saints of all times, these precious believing souls who have endured cruelty and executions. They will be like those who were "tortured or sawn in two" in the verses of God's heroes of faith (Hebrews 11:35–37). We empathize with those who endure to the end of their earthly lives only to be martyred (Revelation 18:2, 24).

The Old Testament Saints, Living and Serving in the Kingdom

Oh, the meeting and fellowship we will have of sharing life stories with the saints of old! It will be fantastic to listen to the stories from righteous people of the early Bible days and the faithful heroes in Hebrews 11. They will tell the rest of the story of their trust and faith in the Almighty, covenant-keeping Jehovah God. They will love to testify to the faithfulness of God in their lives. Praise be to God in psalms and hymns and spiritual songs!

Old Testament Forefathers

As we read about the twelve tribes of Jacob in the Old Testament, these tribes will be existing in the Millennium and will have inheritance property in the Holy Land. Old Testament saints will possibly supervise and be leaders of these same Jewish tribes. We read all of this in the latter part of the book of Ezekiel. The Levite tribe will have property next to the Millennial Temple but will be limited in taking part in the sacrificial system (Ezekiel 44:13; 48:11). The Zadokite priests (a certain tribe of the Levites) will take over that capacity of the brazen altar of burnt sacrifices at the Temple worship (Ezekiel 44:15).

Inheritance of Property

The dividing up of the allotment of the tribes of Judah, Simeon, Naphtali, Dan, and Gad to the north will stretch from Egypt to the Euphrates River (Ezekiel 48). In Ezekiel, we read the prophecies concerning these prescribed landmasses of property. There will be a renewed interest and surveyed inheritance given again to each of the twelve tribes (Ezekiel 48:1–29). The measurements of the tribe of Judah will be twenty-five thousand cubits wide by twenty-five thousand cubits long. This landmass will have included the capital city (Jerusalem) and an allotment of the Levi priests to work at the Millennial Temple (vv. 8–22).

At the end of Ezekiel's prophecies, there are three gates on each square side of Jerusalem (Zion), which depict the twelve sons of Jacob. Even Joseph's name is stated here on one of the gates (Ezekiel 48:32). He is one of Jacob's original and special lineup of sons. Honor is due to the excellent leadership Joseph had in saving the then-known world from hunger in Egypt (Acts 7:9–13). Why is Joseph now named here in this passage? It is because the twelve names are contributed to gates and not an inheritance of a landmass. Levi's descendants were not given a region for settling in the "Promise Land" as twelve tribes. The previous statements of scripture have Manasseh and Ephraim (the sons of Joseph) to occupy property inheritance, rather than listed as Joseph himself (Joshua 16:1–4; Ezekiel 48:4–6).

King David as Prince

We read about King David being there in Jerusalem. Ezekiel 37:25 states, "My servant David shall be their prince forever." There will be a "prince" ruling and reigning in the capital city of Jerusalem. This "prince" will be a descendent of David in flesh and blood, ruling as mayor (Ezekiel 44:3; 45:7; 48:22). Dr. John Walvoord and Dr. Roy Zuck studied various passages to describe David by name in a future restoration of Israel (Jeremiah 30:9; Ezekiel 37:24–25; Hosea 3:5).

Ezekiel indicated that David would be the prince (*nāśî'*) of the Jewish people" (Ezekiel 34:23–24; 37:25). This same "prince" will offer sin offerings for himself during the millennial period (45:22; 46:4). Such actions would hardly be appropriate for the sinless Son of God, but they would be for David.[51]

It seems that this is a literal reference to a resurrected David. So, King David, in his glorified body, will be governing in Zion. This "prince" described in Ezekiel is not the same as the "Prince of Peace" mentioned in Isaiah 9:6, who was Jesus. Jesus will indeed be bringing peace to His Kingdom, but all indications of the "prince" (as the city's mayor) living in and around the Temple court area are different than the place Jesus the King will have in His throne room. Imagine all the revisions and remodeling Jerusalem will have by the time the Kingdom comes to an end. Praise the Lord for all He will do and accomplish for His glory and honor. Alleluia and amen!

CHAPTER 13

KING JESUS WILL REIGN IN GLORY FROM HIS THRONE IN ZION

And they shall call you "the City of the LORD,"
Zion of the Holy One of Israel.
—Isaiah 60:14

Zion (zī′uhn) is a Hebrew word that means a "citadel" or "fortress." According to 2 Samuel 5:6–10, King David and his men took Zion (Jerusalem) from the Jebusites. They may have climbed through a water tunnel or shaft and opened the city gate from the inside. Second Samuel 5:7 states that "David took the stronghold of Zion, that was called the 'City of David.'" The names "Jerusalem," "Zion," and the "City of David" are synonymous throughout scripture.

King David, son of Jesse, was a warrior and saw that Mount Moriah (Zion or Jerusalem, the height of 105 feet) was a citadel pike to be his fortress in building the city. Various valleys surrounded it, except for on the north section. Zion is called "His (God's) holy mountain, beautiful in elevation, the joy of the whole earth, is Mount Zion on the sides of the north, the city of the great King" (Psalm 48:1–2).

Zion became David's fortress from the enemies and a place for him to build his palace and protect His kingdom. It became "the city of David" (1 Kings 8:1; 14:21; 2 Kings 19:21, 31). In the later books of the Old Testament, the name "Zion" denotes Jerusalem (Psalm 87:2, 5; 149:2; Isaiah 33:14; Joel 2:1) and sometimes God's chosen people, Israel (Psalm 51:18; 87:5).

The Psalms exalt the qualities of Zion and themes, as "my [God's] holy hill" (Psalm 2:6) and "the holy place of the tabernacle of the Most High" (Psalm 46:4). It is "Mount Zion which he loves," where God "built his sanctuary like the highest heights" (Psalm 78:68–69). The city of Jerusalem was a holy place because of the presence of God's temple.[52] Praise the Lord on High! This same city has been the capital of God's holy people and His land. God will exalt Zion as a summit citadel for King Jesus, seated and crowned for the Millennial Kingdom.

The Ruling Personnel in their Specialties of Assignments and Duties

And blessed be His glorious name forever! And let the whole earth be filled with His glory. Amen and Amen. (Psalm 72:19)

Just think of King Jesus sitting on His throne and ruling and reigning from His throne room. It will be his divine palace and court of justice in Zion. His throne "will be high and lifted up" (Isaiah 6:1–5). There will be other thrones, which we have seen from the book of Revelation, with the saints ruling with Him. Jesus's throne will be magnificent! His throne will be the center of His arena of majesty. His brilliance and splendor will light up the whole palace. It is a place of 24-7 activity of the ruling saints coming and going from his courts. Many will surround His kingship and His loving counsel of wisdom. He will distribute responsibilities and duties to the saints.

Our King Jesus, in His resurrected body, will not have to sleep. Likewise, the saints in their glorified bodies will not have to sleep.

(Remember, there will be the same sun as we know of it today. So, there will be the darkness of night on half of the earth as it spins on its axis). The saints may rule during the day to oversee the human workers. At nighttime, the supervisors may come to Zion, the King's courtroom, for further instruction, consultation, and mandates to perform in various regions and countries around the world.

King Jesus in Full Control

As we mentioned before from the parables, Jesus said that God's Church saints will be governors and mayors of cities around the world. They may come back to Jerusalem for seminars, instructions, or worship, promoted and mandated by Jesus. Leaders around the world will communicate with each other, and nothing will escape the omniscient character of our God.

King Jesus Will Designate Management

Jesus will give managerial duties and responsibilities to those He chooses. He would have given crowns of reward and authority at the Bema Seat judgment to the Church saints already in heaven. Then He will give out their specialized work areas of supervision in the Millennium. The Old Testament saints, along with the Tribulation saints will be given their designated responsibilities right after the Marriage Supper of the Lamb.

1. Management of Peace: There will be no war or uprising against the rulership of King Jesus. Yet we read that, by the end of the millennial reign, there will be final deceit from Satan to bring the children of believing families (Note: These children may be unbelievers.) into contempt of Jesus's rule (Revelation 20:8). There may be a police force to maintain peace and order during

this Kingdom's reign. There will not be bullets or guns during the Millennium. King Jesus will have His way of peaceful solutions to any rebellion against His leadership.

Even now, there are taser guns to shock people so that the policeman can handcuff an assailant. Something like a taser gun may be used in the Kingdom to bring rebellious children into an alliance with the King and His majesty. It will be true in the future as in our time of grace now, that some worship God outwardly, but inwardly not be in subjection to the Lord. There will be hypocrites then as even now in the Church. These disobedient future children and parents, also of believing flesh and blood families, will be sought after and counseled directly during this Kingdom age.

King Jesus will have management and directors over the peace and order of His Kingdom for a thousand years. "David My servant (Jesus) shall be king over them, and they shall all have one shepherd; they shall also walk in My judgments and observe My statutes and do them" (Ezekiel 37:24).

2. Management of Agriculture and Marketing: With the advantages of agrarian technology, Jesus will designate specialists over the farming communities. Such specialization will be with orchards, greenhouses, warehouses, and supermarkets to distribute the wealth of God's crops and harvests. There will be billions of people to feed in the thousand years of a growing population around the world. It just makes sense that King Jesus will be officiating the management and economy issues with key personnel in all aspects. He will have the best wisdom and balance in the various regions around the world. He was, is, and will still be the Creator of all global growth and goods. How can we ever think less of Him? Praise be to the God who provides all our daily bread!

3. Management of Commercial Economics: The scriptures do not mention the form of currency during the Millennial Kingdom. Maybe there will be no coins or bills as we know of them today. Perhaps credit cards or SIM card chips under the skin will be used as they were during the Tribulation time. It will not be difficult to work

out one source and one kingdom of commerce around the world. At this point, we have no idea what that will be like in the Kingdom Age. The King will set up the banks of its day with or without Wall Street or the stock market.

4. Management of Pharmaceutical Medicines: As we mentioned earlier, the scripture talks about fruit trees, irrigational waters, and healing in the streams. Medications will be researched and used for sick people around the world. From the sanctuary of God of Jerusalem, with its plants and trees, there will be healing for the nations. "Along the bank of the river, on this side and that, will grow all kinds of trees used for food; their leaves will not wither, and their fruit will not fail. They will bear fruit every month because their water flows from the sanctuary. Their fruit will be for food and their leaves for medicine" (Ezekiel 47:12).

Scientists will invent medicines from leaves, roots, nuts, and fruits. King Jesus will help bring about the natural formulas that will bring healing to many people. Jesus may not automatically heal everyone, but long life is prophesied. Seminars will be given and taught about eating healthy for longevity during the Millennium. King Jesus will promote health for all living creatures on the earth.

5. Management of Factories and Construction: We have learned that war implements, guns, tanks, and missiles will be recycled back to furnaces to make new steel and metals. From the metal, they will make farming plows and construction materials. There will be factories of all kinds for labor-saving appliances and machines like we have now. Cities will be built with the latest technology. The magnificent Jerusalem temple will be brilliantly constructed. The Temple has specified dimensions given in Ezekiel 41–44. There will be so much accomplished in the Millennium by many types of specialists. Jesus Himself will put them in their rightful places as administrators, managers, and foremen, according to their gifts and abilities.

The Ruling Priests during the Time of the Kingdom for the Glory of God

"And I will also take some of them for priests and Levites," says the LORD. (Isaiah 66:21)

In the Temple Mount of Zion, the place of the King's holy hill, the Millennial Temple will stand in all its superb elegance and glory. It will radiate from its high-structured walls, chambers, and gates. It is God's holy sanctuary. In Ezekiel 40–43, God describes to the prophet Ezekiel the splendor and majesty of this magnificent temple. The sacred altars will be reproduced and placed in position as in Solomon's Temple, yet more significant in size. The old Hebrew set of "rods and cubits" will be used as measurements. Estimates will exceed that of the first plans given at the time of King David and King Solomon. The spacious dimensions provide more extensive areas of courts, priestly chambers, tables, and sacrifice places in preparation for burnt offerings.

God's Glory Fills the Temple

Ezekiel saw from the eastern gate the splendor and holiness of God's glory that filled the holy of holies (Ezekiel 43:1–4). Verse 2 says the sky and "earth shone with His glory." "The Spirit lifted me up and brought me into the inner court; and behold, the glory of the LORD filled the temple" (Ezekiel 43:5). This glorious entrance will initiate a start again of the sacrificial Jewish customs, likened to the Old Testament ceremonies and rituals. God's glory will fill the holy sanctuary upon the completion of the Temple. The Jewish rituals and practices will bring remembrance of Christ's final and perfect sacrifice of laying down His life on the cruel cross of Calvary. Believers of all times have trusted Christ's blood alone for their redemption.

Similar Duties as in the Time of Aaron

The priestly duties of the Millennium will be comparable to the Levitical priesthood, as they cared for the Temple in the Old and New Testaments. The offering for the sacrificial substitution for sin on the altar will be identical to that of the Old Testament. They will wear their holy garments and turbans as described in the writings of Moses. Most likely, the same sort of design with tassels will also be introduced again in the Millennium. Many of Ezekiel's words of God's future instruction is comparable to the Tabernacle in the time of Moses and Aaron in Exodus 28.

When we continue to read the description of the priests in Ezekiel 44, we find that the priests will minister in the Millennial Temple in the same way it was described in the Pentateuch. God has promised a land area for the holy Temple Mount as an inheritance for the Levite tribe. The Levites will live in the vicinity of the Temple. Just as the Levites lived closest to the Tabernacle during the wilderness journeys, so will these workers of God's Temple be closely accessible to their duties at the Millennial Temple.

Inheritance of the Twelve Tribes

In Ezekiel 45 and 48, there is a dividing up of a heritage of land among the twelve sons of Jacob. The area for the twelve tribes will be divided equally in the Holy Land by survey engineers. Each will be twenty-five-thousand-cubit distance east to west (around twelve kilometers) by thirteen hundred meters (1.3 kilometers) north and south (Ezekiel 48:9–10). Ezekiel gives the dimensions of the Temple Mount in the territory of the Levitical region.

These Levitical priests will serve as Aaron and his sons did in the Tabernacle in the wilderness. Their descendants continued to serve in that way in the Promised Land of Canaan and beyond. They were the ministering servants of the priests' work around the Temple.

Their duties included putting out the holy showbread, lighting the oil lamps, changing the incense, and offering the bulls, goats, and sheep for peace, grain, and burnt offerings on the brazen altar. Levite property was adjacent to the Temple's designated area (south). It brought a sacrificial sweet aroma unto the Lord God (Leviticus 23:18).

Levite Duties Change

In Ezekiel 44, God reveals the duties and responsibilities of the Levitical priesthood. It tells what the priests will do during the millennial reign of Christ. During the time of unrighteous kings of Judah in the past, the Levites made ungodly compromises in the priestly care of the Temple. They did not keep the Law or fulfill all the duties given by God in keeping the holy instruments, court area, and sacred entrances of the Temple (Leviticus 22:2). God spoke to Ezekiel to write these words:

> And the Levites who went far from Me, when Israel went astray, who strayed away from Me after their idols, they shall bear their iniquity. (Ezekiel 44:10)

An explanation of the Levite priest's sin is found in Ezekiel 44:12–13 and Numbers 16:9, 40:

> Because they ministered to them before their idols and caused the house of Israel to fall into iniquity, therefore I have raised My hand in an oath against them," says the LORD GOD, 'that they shall bear their iniquity.'" "And they shall not come near Me to minister to Me as a priest, or come near any of My holy things, or into the Most Holy Place, but

they shall bear their shame and their abominations
which they have committed (44:12–13).

Now, what will these Temple Levites do in the Millennium?
They will serve King Jesus and the high priests:

> Yet they shall be ministers in My sanctuary, as
> gatekeepers of the house and ministers of the house.
> (Ezekiel 44:11a)

I wonder if they will minister in the court areas or as the keepers
of the house of the prince who lives next to the Temple?

> They shall slay the burnt offering and the sacrifices
> for the people, and they shall stand before them to
> minister to them … Nevertheless, I will make them
> keep the charge of the Temple, for all its work, and
> all that has to be done in it. (Ezekiel 44:11b,14)

Levites as Temple Helpers

It is as if God is going back to the original description of all
the works and ministry that the Levites were assigned to do in the
Tabernacle. In Exodus 26, God instructed the tent construction
of the wilderness Tabernacle. In the past, they had packed up,
dismantled, and mantled the structure and skins used in the LORD's
tent of meeting (Exodus 40:2).

Numbers 3:17ff gives detailed commandments and distribution
of work for the sons of Levi. His sons were Gershon, Kohath, and
Merari. Moses wrote down what each of these sons and their sons
after them would have to be responsible for in ministering in God's
Holy Tabernacle. Later, there was also a distribution of duties for the
descendants of Levi in Solomon's Temple. Numbers 3 states that all

the Levites from thirty years old to fifty were to render service to the Lord. Yet, if they got near forbidden places, they would die. Verse 20 makes it clear that they were to stay confined to the assignments God had given them.

Aaron and his sons, as acting high priests, would be the only ones who would manage the final arrangement of the holy items in the holy places. The Levites had a designated and essential part of ministering in the Tabernacle of the meeting. The Levites will also serve and minister in the Millennial Temple to come.

Zadokites as the High Priests

Who are the priests who God will honor to minister to Him at the altar of incense and altar of burnt offerings in the Millennial Kingdom? The descendants of Zadok's family will be the high priests in the Millennium.

> For the priests, the Levites, the sons of Zadok, who kept the charge of My sanctuary when the children of Israel went astray from Me, they shall come near Me to minister to Me, and they shall stand before Me to offer to Me the fat and the blood, says the LORD GOD. They shall enter My sanctuary, and they shall come near My table to minister to Me, and they shall keep my charge. (Ezekiel 44:15–16)

In the Levite line of offspring, there was the family of Zadok, who stayed faithful and righteous before the LORD. The descendants of Zadok will be the chosen family members who will wave the offerings and place the sanctified pieces of the animal sacrifices and grain offerings on the brazen altar during the Millennium. They also will burn the incense in the holy place of the Temple. The Zadokites will be the mediating priests (just like Aaron and his sons were) before the Lord during the thousand years of Christ's reign.

Note: Leviticus 23:14–20 mentions that only the high priest or the one in line to be the next high priest would be allowed to approach the brazen altar to have a wave offering for the Sabbath or feast days. There were to be first-fruit peace offerings of grain and two male lambs that the special priest would wave to lift unto the Lord. He would wave that offering to the Lord God just before he would place it on the flames of the altar. The Zadokite priests will do this in the Millennium time to come.

Why the Change in High Priests?

For a clearer understanding of the judgment on the Levite tribe, read 2 Kings 22–23. King Josiah wanted to correct the abomination of Baal worship that had crept into Jerusalem and Judah. They had beautified other hillsides and valleys for the idolatrous servitude that made God jealous. He does not want any competition of images made that take the place of full devotion to Him alone. The family of Zadok will be the ministering priests and high priests who will represent men to God in this regained Jewish sacrificial system. Ezekiel 44 explains this dilemma and change of status of ministering priests in the Millennial Temple.

CHAPTER 14

THE GLORIOUS TEMPLE
WHERE ALL PEOPLE WILL
WORSHIP THE JEHOVAH GOD

In the Last Days, the mountain of the LORD's Temple
will be established as chief among the mountains; it will
be raised above the hills, and peoples will stream to it.
—Micah 4:1

The Vision of the Millennial Temple

In Ezekiel 40, God took Ezekiel back to Jerusalem in a vision
(resembling the vision in Ezekiel 8:1–3). Jerusalem would be
vastly different from what it was before. Ezekiel's "tour" of
the future Temple is recorded in remarkable detail. This tour was
given by a figure of a man, probably an angel. Yet most likely, he is
the preincarnate Christ whose appearance was like bronze (Ezekiel
40:3). Daniel 10:5–6 adds that His eyes were like torches of fire.

Ezekiel was to "declare to the house of Israel (the Israelites)
everything you see" (Ezekiel 40:4) and write what God has revealed
to him. The Millennial Temple was positioned east and west.
Naturally, with the sun rising over the Mount of Olives, the eastern

gate would be the first description given to Ezekiel to write the overall dimensions. And just a note here that the "glory of the Lord" left the Temple Mount to travel out of the eastern gate off to the Mount of Olives, to its heavenly abode (Ezekiel 10:4, 18–19; 11:22–23). The same "glory of the Lord" will return to the Millennial Temple to dwell (Ezekiel 43:2, 4–5).

The Outer Court of the Temple (Ezekiel 40:5–27)

In the bronze "man's hand was a measuring rod (stick) six cubits long, each being a cubit and a handbreadth" (Ezekiel 40:5). In Ezekiel's time, a common cubit was about eighteen inches long, and a long cubit (with another six inches for a regular width of a man's hand) was about twenty-one inches long. And the measuring rod was approximately about ten and a half feet in length. Therefore, the wall surrounding the Temple was ten and a half feet (one rod) thick and one rod high (v. 5). [53]

The Eastern Gate (Ezekiel 40:6–16)

This angelic man leads Ezekiel to the eastern gate. That man measured the width as the one-rod length of the threshold of the gate (v. 6). The steps, the inlets, or vestibules of such were like alcoves for the guard's chambers. There were three vestibule chambers just inside the east gate. The entrance to the gateway itself was ten cubits, and the length of the gate was thirteen cubits (v. 11). All these dimensions are written down in these verses for these sorts of porches with decorative palm trees on the gateposts. There were beveled window frames and archways over much of the structure of the eastern entrance to the outer court of the Millennial Temple (v. 16).

The Other Two Gates of the Outer Court (Ezekiel 40:17–27)

Entering the outer court, Ezekiel saw a pavement (maybe a tile sidewalk). Yet, moving forward was a spacious larger area of tiling and glamour of landscape ... All around this outer court, were thirty rooms (chambers) along the pavement against the outer wall. These rooms were spaced equally in number along the north, east, and south walls of the Temple. (Ezekiel 40:17–19; see the sketch "The Millennial Temple")

We do not know how they used these rooms, but they may have been storage rooms or meeting rooms for the people when they celebrated their feasts (Jeremiah 35:2). The distance from the inside of the lower gateway (the east gate) to the gate leading to the inner court was 175 feet (100 cubits or 53 meters)."[54]

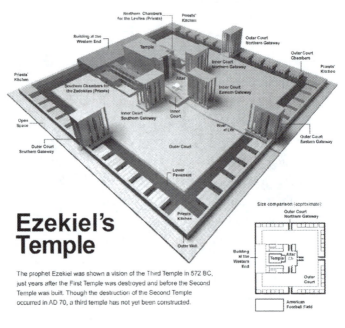

Ezekiel's Temple

The prophet Ezekiel was shown a vision of the Third Temple in 572 BC, just years after the First Temple was destroyed and before the Second Temple was built. Though the destruction of the Second Temple occurred in AD 70, a third temple has not yet been constructed.

GRAPHIC BY KAPOOL MULTIMEDIA. COPYRIGHT 2008 LOGOS BIBLE SOFTWARE

Ezekiel was led from the east gate of the outer court to the north gate (Ezekiel 40:20–23) and the south gate (Ezekiel 40:24–27). Both gates were identical to the eastern gate. There is no west-facing gate. God prepared the contractors and builders with specified dimensions given in His Holy Word.

The Three Gates to the Inner Court (Ezekiel 40:28–47)

After measuring the outer court, the angel measured the inner court. He went from the south gate of the outer court through the south gate of the inner court. This gate had the same measurements as the others. The south gate (Ezekiel 40:28–31), east gate (Ezekiel 40:32–34), and north gate (Ezekiel 40:35–37) of the inner court were identical and were also the same as the three gates of the outer court except that the porches of the inner gates faced the outer court. The porch or vestibule faced the other direction on these gates.

At the inner gates, tables were set up for the preparation of the sacrifices. "Four tables were on one side and four on the other side" in the inner court (Ezekiel 40:41). Thus, eight tables total to have the flesh of the animal sacrifices prepared and ready for the high priests to lay on the brazen altar.

Some people wonder about the idea of animal sacrifices renewed during the Millennium. They think sacrifices were only a part of the Old Testament Levitical Law. Many take the passage symbolically rather than literally. No difficulty is present if we understand the function of these sacrifices. First, animal sacrifices never really pardoned men's sin; only the sacrifice of Christ can do that (Hebrews 10:1–4, 10). In the prior dispensation, Israelites still were saved by grace through faith. The sacrifices only helped restore a believer's relationship with God. Secondly, even after the beginning of the Church Age, Jewish believers still sacrificed to worship at the Temple (Acts 2:46; 3:1; 5:42; 21:26). In the Millennium, believers will view the sacrifices as memorials to Christ's death.

As Jesus said, the New Testament saints are to remember His body and blood until He comes again into His Kingdom. He would "not drink of the fruit of the vine until the kingdom of God comes" (Luke 22:16–18). The remembrance of the Lord's Supper is only for the Church Age to "proclaim the Lord's death till he comes" (1 Corinthians 11:25–26).

The renewed sacrificial system will be reinstituted throughout all the Millennial Kingdom years. God will move away from Church and Tribulation emphasis to the benefits to the Gentiles to Christ's millennial reign. "The fullness of the Gentiles has come in" or been accomplished (Romans 11:25–27). "The Redeemer will come to Zion" (Isaiah 59:20–21). The Lord God's Millennial Temple will be built, and animal sacrifices will display the reminder of Christ's supreme sacrifice in taking the "penalty of sin" on the cross. (2

Corinthians 5:21). Jesus's atoning sacrifice "once for all" (Hebrews 10:10). There are other prophetic Old Testament passages that mention sacrifices in the Millennium.

> Even them I will bring to My holy mountain … their burnt offerings and their sacrifices will be accepted on My altar. (Isaiah 56:7; Isaiah 66:20–23; Zechariah 14:16–21; Malachi 3:3–4)

The tour continued for Ezekiel to enter the inner court area gates. There were two rooms, one at the side of the north, facing south, and another at the side of the south, facing north. The room on the north side was for the caretaker priests of the Temple. The room on the south side was for the high priests who sacrificed the offerings on the brazen altar. These rooms served as storage areas for equipment and rest areas for those priests with responsibilities at the Temple. As stated before, these priests at the altar will be descendants of Zadok (Ezekiel 43:19; 44:15; 48:11), the high priest from Solomon's day (1 Kings 1:26–27). Zadok even anointed Solomon as king in his day along with prophet Nathan (1 Kings 1:34). [55]

As we close off this section on the Millennial Temple's site, dimensions, and sacrificial offerings dedicated and presented to the Lord God, we can anticipate with excitement that glory will be given to the God of gods and King of kings. You, as the reader, should read these last chapters of Ezekiel carefully to know and verify in your mind that there is a literal, earthly Kingdom to come and a spectacular Temple to honor our Lord God. It will be a whole new future "down the road," an outlook and a hope to be there for a revived Temple worship. The excitement will be for the millennial celebrations to our Savior, Jesus. Amen and amen! Are you ready to be there?

The Revelation of the Celebrated Feasts

The Passover and Unleavened Bread Combined

In Ezekiel 45:18–25, there will be a time at the first day of the first month of the Jewish calendar whereby there will be cleansing for the priests personally and the Temple. It is a preparation for the celebration of the Passover feast (Ezekiel 45:21–24) including the Feast of Unleavened Bread. These two feasts are celebrated on the same occasion. The Passover will last seven days, during which the people will eat bread made without yeast. There will be a plastering of blood on the doorposts of the Temple, altar, and inner gateposts of the inner court. It is a remembrance of the hyssop of blood on the doorposts of houses in Egypt as when God sent the last plague. At that time, if the death angel did not see the blood when he passed over, death came to the firstborn of each family—and even Pharaoh's house. What a shame, but God's grace and provision saw the "blood" as a covering for each family. They had a choice to follow God's instructions to apply the blood or not.

The Festival of Tabernacles

In Zechariah 14:16–19, the Feast of Tabernacles is the third feast, which will begin in the seventh month on the fifth day. It also is a seven-day celebration (Leviticus 23:33–44), which is the last feast in Israel's yearly calendar. Why did Ezekiel omit Israel's other national feasts such as the Feast of Pentecost, the Feast of Trumpets, and the Day of Atonement? He may have been signaling a change in God's program for Israel. The inauguration of the New Covenant and the fulfillment of Israel's kingdom promises may render those three feasts unnecessary. Only three of the six annual feasts under the Levitical system (Leviticus 23:4–44) will be followed. The two feasts celebrating national cleansing (Passover and Unleavened Bread) are combined as one feast, which will point back to Christ's death. The last, but not least, Jewish festivity will be the "Feast of Tabernacles" which will enthusiastically be in Zion to glorify and honor the King (Zechariah 14:16, 20–21).[56]

In Jeremiah 3:14–17, there is this interpretation of the millennial city of Zion. It could also be describing what the New Jerusalem will be like for people gathered to God's dwelling place.

> At that time Jerusalem shall be called the "Throne of the LORD," and all the nations shall be gathered to it, to the name of the LORD. (Jeremiah 3:17)

There may be representatives and families coming from all over the globe to this yearly Feast of Tabernacles. A further study of Leviticus 23 explains that people coming to the Holy Mount will cut down palm branches and sticks to build booths or coverings to claim a space around Jerusalem for the festival time.

Zechariah's prophecies for the Millennium speak of families from every nation who will come and worship the King, "the LORD of hosts" (Zechariah 14:16). They will keep the Feast of Tabernacles. If they do not come, there will be a plague of drought and famine against them. Egypt is an example of a plague as punishment that will come upon those peoples and nations who do not make the pilgrimage to celebrate (Zechariah 14:16–19).

I am looking forward to that millennial time to view all the worshippers coming to feast and enjoy the adoration and praise to King Jesus for a week of celebration.

CHAPTER 15

THE VERY LAST REBELLION AND THE BATTLE OVER EVIL

Let them praise the name of the LORD, for His name
alone is exalted; His glory is above the earth and heaven.
—Psalm 148:13

s the millennial reign of the majestic, almighty, and
honorable God, King Jesus will come to the close of His
thousand-year kingdom, there will be a final battle against
the wicked one, Satan (Revelation 20:7–10). King Jesus will, for
the duration of the Millennium will stop all uprisings that sinful
men and women have against His authority. His police force and
communication from His throne will restrain rebellion. Peace will
reign in every nation, province, and city across the globe.

Satan Released to Deceive the Nations

As the revelation of God's Holy Scriptures has depicted, there
is the last battle at the end of the Millennium. God will allow
the old serpent dragon, Satan, to come back from the bottomless
pit to deceive the gullible people in the world. It is not clear from
Revelation 20 how many weeks or months God will allow Satan

to roam around the various nations to make a final try of rebellion against King Jesus. There are only four verses to explain this evil plot and deception:

> Satan will be released from his prison and will go out to deceive the nations which are in the four corners of the earth, Gog and Magog, to gather them together to battle, whose number is as the sand of the sea. They went up on the breath of the earth and surrounded the camp of the saints and the beloved city. And fire came down from God out of heaven and devoured them. The devil, who deceived them, was cast into the lake of fire and brimstone where the beast and the false prophet are. And they will be tormented day and night forever and ever. (Revelation 20:7–10)

Satan's Rebellion Ends Up in Defeat

The explanation is simple. Satan will deceive all the hypocritical, insensitive, carnal, and unbelieving rebels who are against the theocratic government of Jesus's Kingdom. They will be tempted, hoodwinked, and banded together to march from the four corners of the world to make shouts of protest to the King in Jerusalem.

Revelation 20 says that the rebels will be burned up from the fire out of heaven that will devour and consume them. God will send down fire from heaven. Their bodies will burn up from the fire, and their souls will be sent to hell to join with the other dreadful sinners. They will be sent to the lake of fire. This is the last judgment of God. They will stand before Him with the books open and experience the awful "second death" of being cast into the "lake of fire" (Revelation 20:13–15). Satan and all unbelievers will experience this tragic death (meaning "separation" from God) forever in the tormenting judgment of the lake of fire. Amen and amen! Our God is victorious!

Satan's Final Doom to the Lake of Fire

The evil one, Satan, will meet his final match with the Almighty God of the universe. He intends to have the last straw of deceit and protest to the chosen King of Mount Zion. That "serpent of old" will try again to raise his pride to make war against God's anointed, seated on His throne (Revelation 20:2). Catastrophe will come upon him finally to his end and destiny.

He will no longer be "that roaring lion seeking whom he may devour" (1 Peter 5:8). His doom and damnation will come assuredly and suddenly, and he will be defeated and cast into the lake of fire, which burns with sulfur and brimstone (Revelation 19:20; 20:10). There will be no more treachery or deceit:

> The LORD rebuke you, Satan! The LORD who
> has chosen Jerusalem rebuke you! (Zechariah 3:2)

No one will ever have to "rebuke" Satan again (Jude 9). Satan has his last deceit and judgment. This old serpent, the devil, "will be tormented day and night forever and ever" (Revelation 20:10). Amen. Praise to the Lord Almighty!

CHAPTER 16

THE AFTERMATH OF THE GLORIOUS MILLENNIUM THAT LIVES ON ETERNALLY

The sun shall no longer be your light by day, nor for
brightness shall the moon give light to you, But the LORD
will be to you an everlasting light, and your God your glory.
Your sun shall no longer go down, nor shall your moon
withdraw itself; for the LORD will be your everlasting
light, and the days of your mourning shall be ended.
—Isaiah 60:19–20

The final rebellion of Satan and his deceived followers will be over, and God will be the victor. Jesus's foes from the rebellion will be burned up and included in the very last judgment of the Lord on all sinners. God, who makes all things beautiful, will judge all who have not met up with His redemptive plan. The sovereign God will fulfill His plan and design for the architecture of a supreme final dwelling for all believers and followers of Him. There is yet a heavenly New Jerusalem to come (Revelation 21). I cannot wait for that special day. Can you?

The New Heaven and Earth

Revelation 21–22 give the next real clues of an eternal state of a new heaven and new earth. The place is from God and for His glory. Jesus talked about this place in John 14:1–3. He will go away and prepare a mansion for us to live in with Him forever. Jesus will create and build a place miraculously for us as is foretold in these closing chapters of the Bible. He will prepare this living space, the "New Jerusalem," for us who have the glamour and beauty of a bride adorned in linen, white and glorious (Revelation 21:2). It will be a place in its orbit with no sun to shine upon it (as we know of it today).

Some have said this "New Jerusalem" city will sit as a giant cube on top of the new earth. The previous old earth will be burned up in a volcanic fire of bursting explosions. It will dissolve and dissipate in outer space (2 Peter 3:10–11). God Himself will be the luminous light in this condominium mansion (Revelation 22:5). Read the last two chapters of Revelation to get the full picture and understand the square footage of the structure filled with God's brilliance.

He is the One coming to live with all His saved saints in the New Jerusalem forever and ever (21:3). The splendor of light will be from "the Lord God" (v. 5). He "is light and in Him is no darkness at all" (1 John 1:5). Jesus will be the light to shine for all in this New Jerusalem cube. John 8:12 states that Jesus is the "Light of the world." There will be no sun or night there:

> The sun shall no longer be your light by day, nor for brightness shall the moon give light to you; But the LORD will be to you an everlasting light; and your God your glory. (Isaiah 60:19).

Isaiah 60:20 goes on to say that there will be no more "mourning." Revelation 21:4 also states that there will be "no more death, or sorrow, crying … or pain, for the former things (of weeping) have passed away." The Lord Jesus, "The Light of the world" (John 8:12), is also the Comforter who "wipes away all our tears" (Revelation 21:4).

God Himself Living with the Saints

Revelation 21:3 expresses the greatness and relational being of God Himself in His holiness with men:

> Behold, the tabernacle of God is with men, and He
> will dwell with them, and they shall be His people.
> God Himself will be with them and be their God.

The eternal God and His Majesty will dwell with His born-again children in the cube of a city, made without human hands. Why do I say a "cube" city?

> The city is laid out as a square; its length is as great
> as its breadth. And he measured the city with the
> reed: twelve thousand furlongs. Its length, breadth,
> and height are equal. (Revelation 21:16)

Is it not true that a cube is equal in length, width, and breadth?

> Then he measured its wall of jewels: one hundred
> and forty-four cubits. (Revelation 21:17)

This would make the size of this New Jerusalem approximately 1,400 square miles. The distance of the United States from north to south is about 1,400 miles. This eternal city and eternal state of all the righteous will have God saved believers living in their condominium mansions.

The Majestic Jerusalem City

God will make this city so majestic and magnificent that it will even outweigh and be more marvelous than the Millennial Kingdom and dominion of Jesus in Zion (Revelation 21:2). How exciting! God will dwell with the saved ones in the New Jerusalem. He will leave His present heaven and live in this vast, majestic city with streets of gold, twelve pearly gates, and twelve foundations, which are named after the twelve apostles. Precious jewels will adorn the gates (21:12). What a spectacular experience!

> And he showed me a pure river of water of life, clear as crystal, proceeding from the throne of God and of the Lamb. (Revelation 22:1)

If we can imagine now, that at the top of this God-made city, there will be His throne room penthouse; from there, a river will flow as clear as crystal down through the middle. This river will have the glamour and excellence of the "tree of life" (Revelation 22:2). There will be twelve kinds of fruits to enjoy (v. 2). Read the last chapters of the Bible to know more about where we will live with God for eternity. Will you be there with me—to live eternally with our Maker and Sovereign God of the Universe?

No Complaints in the New Jerusalem

Who are the critics who say that God is unfair to allow evil and corruption in our world today? They seem to say that He cannot do anything to correct it. The great God and Redeemer will fix all the wrongs and injustice to make His world right. God has spelled out His plan for our eternal state of existence in a New Jerusalem of peace and contentment with Him forever and ever. This dwelling place will have no time clocks or months (there is no orbit of counting the 365 days in a year). It will be a glorious world without end! Praise be to the God who will make all this possible. Jesus, our Lord and King, will be magnified and uplifted as He sits on the penthouse of His glory and glamour on the top of His New Jerusalem mansion.

Proclaiming the Future State

A very appropriate passage proclaims King Jesus as the LORD Almighty:

> This is what the LORD says: Israel's King and Redeemer, the LORD Almighty: I am the first and I am the last; apart from me there is no God. Who then is like me? Let him proclaim it. Let him declare and lay out before me; what has happened since I established my ancient people, and what is yet to come—yes, let him foretell what will come (Isaiah 44:6–7 NIV84).

Can we be God's witnesses to the revealed Holy Scriptures? Can we declare all that has been revealed of Jesus Christ's glorious Millennial Kingdom to come? What a Sovereign Lord God, who will perform all of this. Jesus is exalted from eternity past to eternity future. He has said, "I am the Alpha and Omega, the Beginning and the End …the First and the Last" (Revelation 1:8, 17). His Kingdom will be most glorious to His honorable Majesty. May we praise Him and lift up His holy name on high!

CONCLUSION

So, we, Your people, the sheep of Your pasture, will give You
thanks forever; we will show forth Your praise to all generations.
—Psalm 79:13

The glorious Millennial Kingdom to come will be an
exhilarating life of worship and service to the King of kings
and Lord of lords. The God of the universe and glory will
make every detail of this thousand-year kingdom age marvelous
and spectacular. Were you thrilled in reading about Jesus Christ,
our present Lord, and Savior? Pause now to think about it. He will
become the theocratic ruler of the whole world. What fascinated you
the most about what God's Holy Scriptures have to say about the
inauguration of Jesus as the supreme King?

Are you impressed with the future entrance and visible
appearance of Jesus on His white horse as He triumphs in the battle
of Armageddon? Are you delighted that He will deal with all evil in
opposition to the holiness of His being? Praise the Lord! Jesus judges
the rebels swiftly to their rightful and final destinations. He will
make a peaceful existence for all who join Him in His dominion of
ruling the world from His throne room in Zion.

What did you think of the ideas of the Marriage Feast of the
Lamb? There will be a glorious announcement of Jesus's true Bride to
all the guests attending. Only the ones in right standing with Jesus
will be invited to the reception and the coronation of King Jesus.

Jesus said Himself, "People will come from east and west and north and south and will take their places at the feast in the kingdom of God" (Luke 13:29–NIV84). The NKJV states that the guests from the four directions will "sit down in the kingdom of God." Will you be seated at this feast? I am anticipating sitting around the tables with all the body of Christ, the Church. The gathering with all the resurrected saints who endured the seven years of Tribulation will be glorious and magnificent. God has all things planned out to the letter with His majesty of glory. He will recognize and reward the heroes of faith for their rightful deeds.

Will you be there, my friend? Have you examined yourself for the salvation Jesus offers those who come to Him as an unworthy sinner? Will you be included in all Jesus has to offer in His millennial reign? Just think of all you will miss out on if you are not living right now in a cleansed and righteous life. What we do and how we live for Christ now is so essential. Saints will be rewarded and promoted to be the mayors, governors, and supervisors over those living under the King's authority. Are you up to the challenge of a future life with Christ to worship Him, love Him, and obey Him in anything He asks you to perform?

I hope you got a blessing from the prophecies and scriptures used as we learned about the Kingdom. Are you looking forward to Jesus's Second Advent or are you just dwelling on His First Advent? I think believers focus too much on the past. We also may think too much about the church responsibilities of the present. Yes, for sure, we must fulfill our duties of the Great Commandments and the Great Commission. We need to be worthy stewards of what Jesus will ask of us for His future Kingdom. His Millennial Kingdom is not the church of today or tomorrow. There is a Rapture to come, a reuniting of us as His Bride in heaven, to return to help set up His literal earthly Kingdom. This earth will be revitalized and remodeled. There will be a renewed paradise on this third planet from the sun. Humanity lost God's earthly paradise when Adam and Eve sinned against the Holy God. Right now, we are polluting our skies, waterways, and oceans. The earth will not last much longer because we fail to care for and clean up our planet.

One sure thing about our world today is that there is no peace. Over thousands of years, humans have lived and tried to make governments work with an ideal constitution and treaties of peace, yet there have always been wars and rumors of wars (Matthew 24:6). Some say there is no literal thousand-year Millennial Kingdom yet to come. If there is no Millennium, there would be a continuous man-made spiritual kind of Christ's kingdom from a deist (humanity left on their own to solve their problems without God intervening) point of view. If so, we would only have humans to rely on to make for "peace on earth." Humans and politics in any form have failed repeatedly these many years. Only Christ Jesus will bring lasting peace. Do you believe it? Do you see why the Millennium is so important?

Real hope is in God alone. It is a reality of hope in the perfect theocratic government of Christ ruling the world (Titus 2:13–14). Is your faith in God, who has revealed the future of hope for the world in His Millennial Kingdom?

May we all be blessed in what God has given in the Scriptures. He has given the prophecies that will be fulfilled in the future Millennial Kingdom. He is worthy of our worship now and for eternity. Praise and honor belong to our Lord God, who sits on His present throne in heaven!

> He (Jesus) who testifies to these things says, "Surely I am coming quickly." Amen. Even so, come, Lord Jesus! The grace of the Lord Jesus Christ be with you all. Amen." (Revelation 22:20–21).

Your Response to Be in Christ's Kingdom

I hope you have enjoyed and are thrilled with the excitement of the future Millennial Kingdom of the Lord Jesus Christ. My prayer is that you, as a reader and one interested in Bible prophecy, will personally know the coming King. Do you know Him? Is He in your life and soul? Do you remember a time in your life when God's Spirit came into your heart to save you from your unrighteous deeds and sins (1 Peter 1:11; 3:18; 1 John 4:12–15)? If you confess your sins and trust Christ as your Savior, you can be sure of a place in the Millennial Kingdom. It is a part of the eternal future we can have to be with Jesus the Savior.

Many know the inspiring John 3:16: "That whoever believes in Him should not perish but have everlasting life." The assurance of eternal life is in God's Son, the Lord Jesus Christ:

> And this is the testimony: that God has given us
> eternal life, and this life is in His Son. He who has
> the Son has life; he who does not have the Son of
> God does not have life. (1 John 5:11–12)

This "eternal life" is vital for being with God's plan and God's Son, the Lord, as the coming King. Do you have God's "eternal life" living within you? Salvation is a matter of trusting the promise of God in giving eternal life to His children. Are you or are you not a part of God's family of sons or daughters?

Was there a time in your life when you received Jesus as Savior and Redeemer? There needs to be a born-again experience to become a child of God and be a part of His saved children (John 3:3–6). Receiving Christ is a prerequisite to living with Him in heaven and His Millennial Kingdom.

But as many, as received Him, to them He gave the right to become children of God, to those who believe on His name. (John 1:12)

The Spirit of Himself bears witness with our spirit that we are the children of God. (Romans 8:16)

All of God's promises and rights are true for all who believe and "may enter through the gates of the city" (Revelation 22:14). The last chapters of Revelation tell of the "Great White Throne Judgment" (Revelation 20:12), which includes the names of believers who have trusted Jesus.

Revelation 20 talks of the "Great White Throne Judgment." Whoever's name is not written in the Book of Life will be cast into the eternal "lake of fire" (vv. 12–15). In Revelation 21, the "New Jerusalem" is presented as the abiding place of those whose names are written in the Book of Life. They will dwell with the Triune God and His saints forever. And everyone who enters "shall bring the glory and the honor of the nations into it … but only those who (are included) are written in the Book of Life (vv. 26–27).

In the middle of its street (the New Jerusalem), and on either side of the river, was the tree of life, which bore twelve fruits, each yielding its fruit every month. (Revelation 22:2)

Blessed are those who do His commandments, that they may have the right to the tree of life. (Revelation 22:14).

Truly this indeed is life everlasting with our God and coming King Jesus! Those individuals saved from their sin have their names written in the Book of Life and take of the "tree of life" for eternity in God's presence. Will you be there? Will you enjoy the life given to every believer in God's dwelling place of a new heaven and a new earth (Revelation 21:1)?

Are you thirsty for more assurance at this point in your life? Are you thrilled with the coming of the Lord Jesus to be King? He said three times, in the last chapter of the Bible, "Behold, I am coming quickly" (Revelation 22:7, 12, 20). The urgency of having a right relationship with God and the Savior Jesus whom He has sent is necessary to be included in the glorious Millennial Kingdom to come:

> And the Spirit and the Bride say, "Come!" And let him who hears say, "Come!" And let him who thirsts come. Whoever desires, let him take the water of life freely. (Revelation 22:17).

Do you want more? Do you want to quench the thirst for life? Christ Jesus is the thirst quencher!

If you are not sure and you want to know Jesus Christ as your personal Savior from the punishment of sin in hell, then trust and receive Him today:

> Jesus stood (while He was on the earth in His preaching ministry), and cried out, saying, "If anyone thirsts, let him come to Me and drink. He who believes in Me, as the scripture has said, out of his heart will flow rivers of living water." (John 7:37–38)

In a spiritual sense, there is great satisfaction in coming to Jesus for one's spiritual salvation and the promise of a home in heaven.

The woman at the well in Samaria was ready to receive the gift of living water (in a spiritual sense) when Jesus offered it to her. She clung to every word Jesus spoke and received Him as personal Savior of her sins. She gained the living water for her spiritual and eternal life-giving satisfaction (John 4:7–15). I have been satisfied in Christ for more than fifty years. God's Spirit has reassured me through His Word that I am a child of God and that my name is written in the Lamb's Book of Life.

How about you? You can be sure you will be included in the thousand-year reign of Jesus Christ and be with Him for eternity. If you are not sure, believe and receive Christ Jesus the Lord as your Savior! You can pray something like this

> Lord Jesus, I acknowledge that I am a sinner. I have disobeyed your holy commands and have sinned against your holy character. I know now that Jesus's death and resurrection are the only plan for receiving the gift of eternal life. I believe in Christ and His free offer of the living water of salvation in going to heaven. Please write my name in the Book of Life. I want to enter Christ's heaven and Millennial Kingdom someday. I pray and ask your pardon and forgiveness of my evil deeds to have the real-life saving experience to be in heaven when I die. I thank you from the bottom of my heart. In the name of Jesus, Amen.

After your prayer, have you felt the life-giving, born-again experience to be called a child of God? If so, let a friend or relative know your decision. Mark down this day of your salvation. Please email me at pklumpp@abwe.cc about your decision to follow Christ and your thoughts about this glorious Millennial Kingdom.

APPENDIX 1

The Prophetic Definitions and Meaning of Biblical Words

1. ADVENT. A word used to refer to the coming of Christ Jesus. The First Advent (when He came to earth to live and be our Savior, which we commonly celebrate at Christmas) and the Second Advent (Christ's revelation of Himself to the earth).
2. AMILLENNIALISM. A word meaning "no Millennium." A position on biblical prophecy that holds to no earthly thousand-year reign of Christ in Jerusalem.
3. ANTICHRIST. An imposter of Christ (1 John 2:18; Revelation 13:1–10; 2 Thessalonians 2:3–10). A system in opposition to Christ and assumed to be in the stead of Christ (1 John 4:3).
4. APOCALYPSE. Another name for the book of Revelation from the original Greek word, *Apocrypha*, which means the prophetical revelation to unveil future events.
5. ARMAGEDDON. The battle or war in which the Antichrist will organize against Israel just before the Lord Jesus will defeat the enemies at Mount Megiddo in Israel (Revelation 16).
6. BABYLON. An ancient city. Also, a revised term that means the origin of a system (political, commercial, and moral) used in Revelation 17–18, which will be destroyed. This

system means "confusion." It is Satan's chief thrust for deceit in the world.

7. BEAST. Another name of the Antichrist in the book of Revelation 13:19–20; 20:4 (compare Daniel 7).

8. BRIDE. The Church believers in Jesus Christ, selected from among men and women of every nation, tribe, and tongue between Pentecost and the Rapture (Ephesians 5:23–32; John 3:29; Revelation 19:7–16).

9. BRIDEGROOM. The Lord Jesus Christ (Revelation 19:7–9) as the "Lamb of God" (John 3:29).

10. CHURCH. From the Greek word *ekklesia*, meaning a called-out assembly from the world into the body of Christ; baptized and indwelt by the Holy Spirit (1 Corinthians 12:13).

11. DAY of the LORD. Christ's return to the earth to judge and set up His millennial reign.

12. DAVID'S THRONE. The throne promised to Christ Jesus for His reign upon the earth as the ultimate descendant of King David (Revelation 3:21; 2 Samuel 7:12–17; Luke 1:32—33).

13. DISPENSATIONALISM. A biblical designation of a divine economy (from the Greek word, *Oikonomia*); a commitment from God to men with the responsibility given in a certain period of time and duties.

14. ECCLESIOLOGY. The setting forth of the biblical doctrine of the Church.

15. ESCHATOLOGY. A term indicating the study of the last things (from the Greek word, *eschotos*, meaning "last"). The study of biblical prophecies that God has revealed in His Holy Scriptures.

16. ETERNAL STATE. The beginning of everlasting life, which officially starts after the White Throne Judgment (Revelation 20). That judgment determines the eternal estate

for the unsaved condemned to the lake of fire and the saved to live with God in His New Jerusalem (Revelation 21–22).

17. GENTILE. 1 Corinthians 10:32 divides humanity into three groups: Jew, Gentile, and Christ's Church. Jews and Gentiles (non-Jews) who are born-again believers are included in God's Church.

18. GOG. Gog is usually combined with "Magog," kings or people of the north. Some say they are from Russia.

19. HEAVEN. The third heaven of 2 Corinthians 12:5–8 is the place of God's abode that all saved believers go to upon their death.

20. HELL. The intermediate state of the unsaved dead—to be issued to the lake of fire for eternity to come (Revelation 20:14).

21. ISRAEL. This nation was the descendants of Jacob and his twelve sons (tribes) when his name was changed to Israel ("Prince"). God has made His covenants with this chosen nation and they are precious in His sight (Romans 9:1–5; 11:25–26).

22. JEWS. Jewish people were from the southern kingdom of Judah. The tribe of Judah was named such when the nation of Israel (from King Solomon's time) split into two, forming the southern kingdom and the kingdom of Israel to the north. The Jewish race of Israelites were first given the name of "Jews" from the two first letters of their citizenship of Judeans from "Judah" while they were exiled in Babylon.

23. JUDGMENTS. God's judicial sovereign decision to be just and fair. In future prophecies, God will display His wrath against sinful humanity in the Tribulation times.

24. JUDGMENT SEAT of CHRIST. A judgment for believers, immediately after the Rapture. Another name is the "Bema Seat of Christ." Rewards will be given or lost because of one's obedience to God's commands (2 Corinthians 5:10).

25. KINGDOM. A future aspect related to the prophecy that has to do with Christ's earthly rule in Jerusalem. "Thy kingdom come" (Matthew 6:3). God's will be done in giving Jesus the rightful reign on David's throne in the Millennium.

26. LAKE OF FIRE. This is the final judgment of wicked men, women, and unholy angels in the suffering place, which burns with sulfur and brimstone (Revelation 19:20; 20:15).

27. MARRIAGE OF THE LAMB. This will follow the Rapture of the Church and is the marriage of the Church (the "Bride") to Christ Jesus in heaven.

28. MARRIAGE FEAST. Another name given is the "Marriage Supper of the Lamb" as the reception for the Bridegroom (Jesus) with the His Bride (compare Matthew 25:1–10; Luke 12:36).

29. MARANATHA. "The Lord comes forth." The word's only occurrence is in 1 Corinthians 16:22.

30. MIDTRIBULATIONISM. A distinction within the premillennialists by those who hold that the Rapture will occur in the middle of the future seven-year tribulation.

31. OLIVET DISCOURSE. Recorded in Matthew 24–25, and slightly different in Mark 13 and Luke 21, it was Christ's last prophetic message before the cross and was given on the Mount of Olives.

32. POSTTRIBULATIONISM. The belief of premillennialists who hold that there is only one stage of the Second Coming of Christ. After the Tribulation, Christ will receive His own to Himself and return directly to the earth for his reign in one grand movement.

40. PREMILLENNIALISM. A system of theology that holds that Christ will come before the Millennium and reveal Himself and reign on earth for one thousand years.

41. PRETRIBULATIONALISM. Believers hold that Christ will Rapture or catch away His Church before the Tribulation period (1 Thessalonians 4:13–18; Revelation 4).
42. RAPTURE. The removal of the Church by the return of Christ in the clouds to take them up to heaven to dwell with Him forever (1 Corinthians 15:51–52; 1 Thessalonians 4:13–18).
43. REVELATION. A word descriptive of Christ revealing Himself in a marvelous return of His presence to the earth with power and glory.
44. SATAN. The prideful angel Lucifer whom God judged to become the devil as the evil one who tempts all people on the earth. Another biblical name is the "old serpent" or "dragon" (Revelation 12:9).
45. SECOND COMING. The scripture refers to the term as the visible return of Jesus Christ to the earth to reign in His Millennial Kingdom (Zechariah 14:1–7; Revelation 19–20).
46. SIGNS. The indicators of the frequency of earthquakes, wars, and pestilence before the Second Coming of our Lord Jesus Christ (Matthew 24:4–8).
47. THEOCRACY. Government of a state of a rule directed by God (Hebrew "Theo") Himself.
48. ZION. King David's city of Jerusalem which is the millennial capital (Isaiah 2:3; Psalm 2:6; Romans 11:26).

APPENDIX 2

Thoughts, Summaries, and Excerpts from *Who Owns the Land* by Stanley Ellison and revised by Dr. Charles H. Dyer, 2003.

It is important for us to understand the part that the "promised land" plays in Biblical prophecy. A book that has been helpful to me is *Who Owns the Land* by Stanley Ellison and revised by Dr. Charles H. Dyer. With their permission, I would like to share a few summaries and excerpts from the book.

Chapter 11, page 131ff. In recent months and years, the Middle East has commanded media attention all over the world. Various confrontations are always going on between Israel and the Arabs. God has a "promised land" for His chosen people and descendants from Abraham, Isaac, and Jacob (Genesis 12:7; 13:15; 17:8; 26:3; 28:13). Israel has a divine right to the land promised to these three God-given patriarchs of the Old Testament. The Patriarchs were given as a reconfirmed covenant from God at various times and events, a promise that the land of Canaan would be given to their descendants. It was reaffirmed even to Moses and Joshua. They were to cross the Jordan River and claim it as God's (their) property to occupy.

The second claim to the God-given promise was the Palestinian covenant that was given to Moses and the Israelites, elaborated on in Deuteronomy 28–30. Moses itemized the conditions by which Israel could and would occupy the land. God would show His mercy and grace in returning and restoring a chosen generation in possessing the land forever (Psalm 105:9–11). The Abrahamic covenant was God's unconditional promise to him and his descendants. The Palestinian covenant had conditions to be met and enjoyment to experience in God's timing and fulfillment. There was and still is conflict over the land, but the promise still stands true for the Israelites to possess the promised land. God's covenant will culminate quicker into Israel's governing state, with a mighty restoration leading up to Christ's Millennial Kingdom in the future.

The fulfillment of the divine promise and real estate claims will be in God's time. It will be highlighted in the prophetic unfolding drama in fulfillment of Old Testament prophecies. The promised land will gradually be in the hands of the Israelites governing plan even though other claims and persecutions will come upon them. In the last days and years before Christ's return, the world will be in utter chaos. Yet, with God, all His scriptures are true and right. He monitors all the circumstances of politics, oppression of world powers, and negotiations still undergoing for "peace" in the Middle East countries. As stated in Zechariah 1:10–17, "I am zealous ... for Zion with great zeal." God's invisible chariots have not retired or retreated in patrolling the earth to unfold the structure and glory yet to be expressed to the world. It is yet to be seen that Christ will rule and reign in His control over the whole world for His "Kingdom" to come.

Page 135. The Deuteronomy 30:1–3 conditions were later repeated in many Old Testament passages as in Solomon's emphasis at the Temple dedication. First Kings 8, and 2 Chronicles 6–7 express it so explicitly in King Solomon's prayer. He pleaded with God that if His people would turn from godly living in disobedience and repent to humble themselves, the Lord "would hear from heaven" and forgive (2 Chronicles 7:14). Solomon's prayer continued if they were scattered by God's discipline, God said He would still rescue them and return them to their rightful Holy Land of Palestine (Ezekiel 36). In Ellisen's words: "The same conditions were emphasized by the prophet Joel. Also, in his earliest chapters, he presents a paradigm for restoration both historically and prophetically. The key point was that genuine repentance must precede God's blessings of restoration" (Joel 2:12–19).

Page 136. The chapters in Zechariah come into view also in the Lord Jesus's presence being rejected in the First Advent displayed in chapters 9–11 and His Second Coming and reception of Christ as King in chapters 12–14. "They will look on Him in whom they have pierced" (Zechariah 12:10), "which I was wounded in the house of my friends" (Zechariah 13:6). The Lord will bring His people to an end in "turning to the Lord," with repentance and acknowledgment of the Messiah in deep mourning and lamenting. Actually, seeing the nail-scarred hands will bring about grief and regret in the ones who had crucified Christ. Eyes and hearts will be open to bringing about a spiritual revolution and reception to His rightful throne. Yet, praise be to God, there is a result in restoring His people and land to a momentous occasion of viewing the "Lord of lords, and King of kings" (Revelation 19:16). This will all be on display on that grand and glorious day when the whole world will see Jesus on His victorious white horse, appearing with justice from His throne in Zion!

Who Owns the Land, Stanley Ellisen and updated and revised by Charles H. Dyer: Multnomah Press (1991); Tyndale House Publishers (2003).

BIBLIOGRAPHY OF SOURCES AND CHAPTER CITATIONS

1   Gabriel, Charles H., "O That Will Be Glory," 1928, Used by permission for the Inspiring Hymnal, Sacred Music Publishers, Grand Rapids, MI., 1951, Hymn 501.2

2   *John MacArthur's Study Bible*, 2019, and Ron Rhodes, "The End Times in Chronological Order," Harvest House Publishers, 2012, Eugene, OR; 47; 71–72; 184–185.3

3   *Zondervan Study Bible*, D. A. Carson, editor; Zondervan, 2015, Grand Rapids, MI, 2620.4

4   Walvoord, John F., *Revelation*, edited by Philip E. Rawley and Mark Hitchcock; Moody Publishers, 2011, Chicago, IL. 283.5

5   MacArthur 47; 71–72; 184–185.6

6   MacArthur, 47, 71–72, 184–185.7

7   The English-Greek Interlinear New Testament, NKJV, Logos Research Download, 1 John 3:2.8

8   Walvoord, John F.; Zuck, Roy B.; Dallas Theological Seminary: *The Bible Knowledge Commentary: An Exposition of the Scriptures*, (Vol. 2, 893), Wheaton, IL: Victor Books, 1985, Logos Research Download, Psalm 17:15.9

9   Henry, M., (1994) Matthew Henry's commentary on the whole Bible: complete and unabridged in one volume (1908). Peabody: Hendrickson; and Walvoord, John; *The Revelation of Jesus Christ, 1966*, Revised new printing by Rawley and Hitchcock, 2011; Moody Publishers, Chicago, 341.10

10 Walvoord, 341.11

11   Jeremiah, David, *The Jeremiah Study Bible,* Worthy Publishing, USA, *The Revelation*, 1847.12

12   Walvoord, 704–705.13

13   Lucado, Max, *When Christ Comes;* Word Publishing, Nashville, TN, 1999, p.43.14

14   Walvoord, 491.15

15   Henry, 2468.16

16   *Merriam-Webster.com*, https://www.merriam-webster.com/dictionary/solas. 17

17   Walvoord, 985.18

18   Walvoord, 1569.19

19   Strong, J., *Enhanced Strong's Lexicon.* Index file 3318, Woodside Bible Fellowship.20

20   *Nelson's Quick Reference Topical Bible Index.* Nashville, Tenn.: Thomas Nelson Publishers, 1995, 58.21

21   Nelson, 58.22

22   Walvoord, 968.23

23   Walvoord, 968.24

24   Walvoord.25

25   Joseph M. Stowell, *Kingdom Conflict,* Victor Books, Wheaton, IL., 1985, 72–75.26

26   Stowell.27

27   Walvoord, 972–973.28

28   Wiersbe, Warren W., *Wiersbe's Expository Outlines on the Old Testament,* volume 2, Wheaton, IL, 614.29

29   Walvoord, 973.30

30   Walvoord.31

31   Keener, Craig S., *The IVP Bible Background Commentary: New Testament,* InterVarsity Press, Downers Grove, IL., 1993.32

32   Jeremiah, David, *The Commentary Footnotes of David Jeremiah's Study Bible*, Worthy Media, Inc., 1172.33

33   *Encyclopedia of The Bible*; "Valley of Jehoshaphat, Hebrew Text and Meaning," Bible Gateway.34

34   Barnes, Albert, "Truth According to Scripture," *Notes on the Whole Bible.*35

35   Barnes.36

36   Calvin, John, "Joel 3 Commentary," *Truth According to Scripture.*37

37   Barnes.38

38   Keener.39

39 Wikipedia: Bema, a Greek definition.40

40 MacDonald, William; Farstad, Arthur: *Believer's Bible Commentary: Old and New Testaments*. Nashville: Thomas Nelson (1997) 1299.

41 MacDonald, 1299.42

42 MacDonald, 1299.43

43 Jones, Timothy Paul, PhD, *End Times Prophecy*, Rose Publishing Inc., Torrance, CA, 115.44

44 MacDonald, 2116.45

45 Jamieson, Robert; Fausset, A. R.; Brown, David: *A Commentary, Critical and Explanatory on the Old and New Testaments*. Oak Harbor, WA: Logos Research Systems, Inc.46

46 MacDonald, 211647

47 Walvoord, 946.48

48 Wiersbe, 852.49

49 MacDonald, 2377.50

50 Wiersbe.51

51 Walvoord, 1295.52

52 Radmacher, E. D., Allen, R. B., and House, H. W. (1999). *Nelson's New Illustrated Bible Commentary,* Nashville: T. Nelson Publishers, 680.53

53 Walvoord, 1304.54

54 Walvoord.

55 Walvoord.

56 Walvoord, 1571.

Printed in the United States
by Baker & Taylor Publisher Services